AN ENTRY, AN ENTRY

MY KINGDOM FOR AN ENTRY

JAMES MARSH STERNBERG MD (DR J)
AND
DANNY KLEINMAN

authorHOUSE

AuthorHouse™
1663 Liberty Drive
Bloomington, IN 47403
www.authorhouse.com
Phone: 833-262-8899

Published by AuthorHouse 07/20/2021

ISBN: 978-1-6655-3218-1 (sc)
ISBN: 978-1-6655-3217-4 (e)

CONTENTS

PART ONE: DECLARER PLAY

Chapter 1.   Creating Dummy Entries

Chapter 2. Saving Dummy's Entries

Chapter 3.	Creating and Saving Declarer's Entries

Chapter 4.	Trumps As Entries

PART TWO: THE DEFENSE

Chapter 7.   Dislodging Dummy's Entry

Chapter 8.   Unblock and Discard to Create Entries for Partner

ACKNOWLEDGEMENTS

This book would not have been possible without the help of several friends. Frank Stewart, Michael Lawrence, Anne Lund, Eddie Kantar, and Marty Bergen all provided useful suggestions.

We are forever indebted to Alan Brody, Norman Gore, Dick Recht, Norbert Jay, bridge Hall-of-Famer Fred Hamilton and the late Bernie Chazen, without whose friendship, guidance and teaching we could not have achieved whatever success we have had in bridge.

James Marsh Sternberg, MD   Danny Kleinman, Psephologist

Palm Beach Gardens, FL   Los Angeles, CA

DEDICATION

to **VICKIE LEE BADER**,
whose love and care have
carried me thru these times

— JMS

to **NANCY ANN HECK**,
who plays and teaches
and packs lunches for me so I can eat while I work

to **CHERYL ELIZABETH JACOBS**,
who watches me while I play
and serves me those lunches while I work

and to all the vixen in our lives for whose love we live

— DK

INTRODUCTION

EN-TRY! EN-TRY! My kingdom for an EN-TRY

This little word is vital to every bridge player's thought processes. Especially the final syllable, *try*.

A clear understanding of entries should be a top priority of every bridge player. As soon as the dummy appears, declarer and the defenders alike should start thinking about entries. Declarer must plan the transportation between hand and dummy while the defenders must think how to destroy the links between the two and preserve their own links.

Part One of this book looks at deals through declarer's eyes. Declarer's tools include creating entries to either hand, destroying defender's entries, finessing, ducking and hold-up plays, blocking and unblocking, and forcing the defenders to help him.

Part Two looks at deals through the eyes of the defenders, who use similar techniques, creating and destroying entries, blocking and unblocking, avoiding endplays, overtaking honors, preventing declarer from ducking, and others.

The deals are distributed among several chapters with different themes, but they overlap considerably. Some deals might fit in more than one chapter.

We're sure you will recognize some themes and problems from your own bridge experiences. It's best to anticipate each problem before, not after, it arises.

While reading this book, imagine that you are playing in a team game at IMPs, which means that you shouldn't care much about overtricks or an extra 50 or 100 for down more than one. You're not playing at matchpoints, where it's sometimes right to risk your contract in a greedy quest for overtricks and tops. You may stumble occasionally in the play, but your counterpart in the other room is an expert who "always gets it right." I hope this book will help you see the problems in advance and always get them right.

Although the diagrams show all four hands, you may want to cover up the defenders' hands when you are declarer, and the two unseen hands when you are a defender, so you can try to solve each problem before looking at the entire deal.

PART ONE

DECLARER PLAY

Chapter 1. Creating Dummy Entries

DEAL 1. HIDDEN ENTRIES

To maximize the number of tricks in a suit, declarer normally leads from the hand with the weaker suit up to the hand with the stronger suit. Take stock of the entries to each hand. Aces are sure entries, and so are other honors when the defenders have no higher cards left in a suit. Expert declarers seek hidden entries also.

On this deal, your partner has overbid to 7NT. Did she really think your 2NT rebid following her neutral 2♢ response to your 2♣ opening was based on 31 high-card points instead of the usual 23 HCP or so?

```
                        ♠ 8 5
                        ♡ K 7 4 2
                        ♢ A 5 3 2
                        ♣ 9 7 2
        ♠ 9 6 3 2                        ♠ K 10 7 4
        ♡ 10 3                           ♡ Q 9 5
        ♢ 9 6                            ♢ Q 10 8
        ♣ Q J 10 4 3                     ♣ 8 6 5
                        ♠ A Q J
                        ♡ A J 8 6
                        ♢ K J 7 4
                        ♣ A K
```

You can count only seven top tricks; 3-2 splits in the red suits with both queens on side bring you up to 11, and two spade finesses make 13. Four finesses through East need four dummy entries. Do you see them?

Dummy's ♡7 and ♢5 are *hidden* entries. Take care when leading to dummy's high cards to preserve your precious ♡6 and ♢4. Win Trick 1 with the ♣A (declarer normally plays the higher of equals first), then:

Tricks 2 to 5. Lead the ♡8 to dummy's ♡K, and dummy's ♡2 to take the heart finesse, then cash your high heart and cross to dummy's ♡7.

Trick 6. Take a spade finesse.

Tricks 7 to 10. Lead the ♢7 to dummy's ♢A, and dummy's ♢2 to finesse diamonds, then cash your high diamond and cross to dummy's ♢5.

Tricks 11 to 13. Finesse spades again, then cash the ♠A and ♣K.

Slam dunk! Score up your Grand Slam. Do not tell partner, "Nice bid." Do say sweetly and truthfully, "I don't think they'll bid it in the other room."

1

DEAL 2. THE PERCENTAGES ARE GETTING SMALLER, BUT …

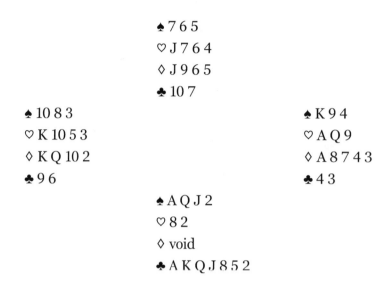

```
                    ♠ 7 6 5
                    ♡ J 7 6 4
                    ◇ J 9 6 5
                    ♣ 10 7
   ♠ 10 8 3                         ♠ K 9 4
   ♡ K 10 5 3                       ♡ A Q 9
   ◇ K Q 10 2                       ◇ A 8 7 4 3
   ♣ 9 6                            ♣ 4 3
                    ♠ A Q J 2
                    ♡ 8 2
                    ◇ void
                    ♣ A K Q J 8 5 2
```

South's 5♣ jump over East's 1◇ opening as dealer bought the contract. Two sure heart losers. One or two spade losers looming: how to avoid losing them?

After ruffing West's ◇K opening lead low, declarer entered dummy with the ♣10 to finesse spades successfully. He drew the outstanding trumps and cashed the ♠A, but when the ♠K did not fall on the second round, he needed spades to split 3-3 just to hold the set to down one … and they did.

"Catching king-third of spades on side is only 18%," said North, "but couldn't you at least try to make the contract even though it was only 9%?"

Why did North think that making 5♣ was only half as likely as the chance of East having ♠Kxx?

In the other room, declaring the same contract, South was willing to risk an extra undertrick to try to make. Needing two entries to finesse spades twice, she ruffed the opening lead with the diamond eight and took an additional finesse against West's club nine. When it succeeded and the spades behaved, she made five clubs.

DEAL 3. YOU LOST A TRICK WHERE?

```
                    ♠ 5 4 3
                    ♡ A K 4 2
                    ◊ Q 8 6 3
                    ♣ 7 6
        ♠ Q J 10 8 2              ♠ 9 7 6
        ♡ J 8 7 6                 ♡ Q 10 9 5 3
        ◊ J 7                     ◊ K 10 9 5
        ♣ 8 3                     ♣ 4
                    ♠ A K
                    ♡ void
                    ◊ A 4 2
                    ♣ A K Q J 10 9 5 2
```

After receiving a positive response to an artificial powerhouse 2♣ opening, South barreled into 6♣. Eleven top tricks in hand, and two top tricks in dummy, but alas, no obvious dummy entry to take even the one more trick required to make 6♣. Or is there?

After capturing West's ♠Q with the ♠A, declarer thought he might reach dummy with the ♣7 on the second round to be able to throw his two low diamonds on North's top hearts.

Alas, when the *eight* of clubs didn't fall under his ♣A, declarer drew the last trump with the ♣K and tried his other chance, leading low to dummy's ◊Q ... which fell to East's ◊K. Down one.

"Sorry partner," said South. "Both my chances failed."

"Guess you didn't want to try the 100% play," replied North, entering minus 100 on his private score.

Can you spot a sure dummy entry?

The declarer in the other room received the same opening lead against 6♣. When she led the ♣2 to West's ♣8 at Trick 2, the defense was helpless. After losing to the ♣8, declarer entered dummy with the ♣7 for the needed diamond discards on North's top hearts.

"Nice play, partner," said North, entering plus 1370 on his scorecard.

"I didn't expect to lose a trump trick with this hand," replied South.

"You wouldn't have, if West had played a lazy three of clubs at Trick Two," said North.

DEAL 4. IN SEARCH OF A DUMMY ENTRY

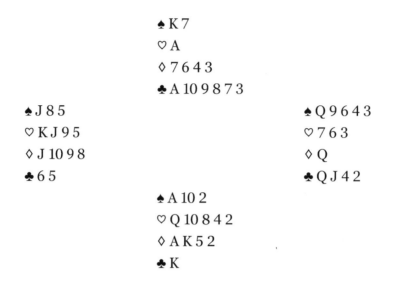

♠ K 7
♡ A
◊ 7 6 4 3
♣ A 10 9 8 7 3

♠ J 8 5
♡ K J 9 5
◊ J 10 9 8
♣ 6 5

♠ Q 9 6 4 3
♡ 7 6 3
◊ Q
♣ Q J 4 2

♠ A 10 2
♡ Q 10 8 4 2
◊ A K 5 2
♣ K

West led the ◊J against South's 3NT. With five top tricks in the other three suits, South needed only four tricks from clubs to make. After unblocking the ♣K, declarer crossed to dummy's ♡A to cash the ♣A and lead a third club. Curtains!

With clubs splitting 4-2 and no honor falling on the first two rounds, declarer lacked the entries to establish and run the rest of dummy's long club suit. Down one.

"Did you expect someone to send a taxi to take you to dummy later?" asked North sarcastically as he marked minus 100 on his scorecard.

How can declarer reach dummy often enough without calling Uber?

In the other room, South showed how. She overtook her ♣K with dummy's ♣A at Trick 2, then led dummy's ♣10 to drive out one of East's stoppers. With two outside entries to dummy and only one more club honor to dislodge, declarer soon had nine tricks.

"Who needs a taxi when a dumb king of clubs can be the horse that will carry you where you need to go?" asked North, chalking up plus 600.

DEAL 5. SECOND SUIT OR TWO FINESSES?

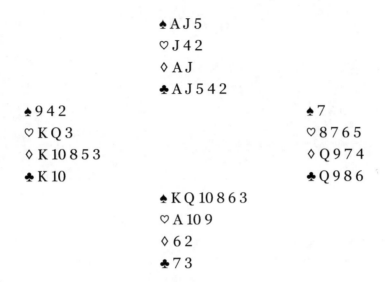

```
                        ♠ A J 5
                        ♡ J 4 2
                        ◊ A J
                        ♣ A J 5 4 2
        ♠ 9 4 2                              ♠ 7
        ♡ K Q 3                              ♡ 8 7 6 5
        ◊ K 10 8 5 3                         ◊ Q 9 7 4
        ♣ K 10                               ♣ Q 9 8 6
                        ♠ K Q 10 8 6 3
                        ♡ A 10 9
                        ◊ 6 2
                        ♣ 7 3
```

South opened a classic Weak 2♠ Bid as dealer and North's 4♠ raise ended the auction. Though a tempting ♡K opening lead would have given declarer his needed tenth trick, West's ◊5 lead left declarer one trick short.

Declarer took dummy's ◊A and drew trumps in three rounds ending in dummy. He played to catch at least one heart honor on side, finessing twice. Not bad, succeeding 75% of the time, but not today. Down one.

Unlucky? Yes, but was there a better plan?

In the other room, his counterpart saw one. A 4-2 club split could let him set up one long club for a tenth trick; a 3-3 club split could yield an overtrick. The combined chances, 48% and 36%, totaled 84%. That's better than 75%.

To bring the clubs home might require three dummy entries: two to ruff clubs and one to reach the good club. South had to save the club ace until he was ready to ruff a club. At Trick Two, he ducked a low club to West's ♣10. West cashed the ◊K, but declarer was in control.

He won West's trump exit in hand and led a club to dummy's ♣A. He ruffed a club high, crossed to dummy's ♠J, and ruffed another club high. A trump to dummy's ♠A drew West's last trump and dummy's fifth club provided a tenth trick.

DEAL 6. ONE MORE ENTRY, PLEASE

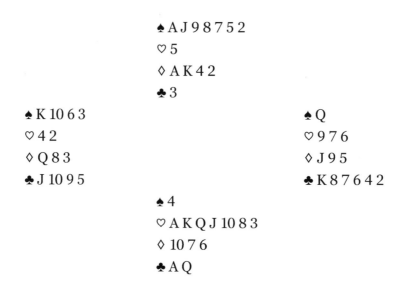

```
                    ♠ A J 9 8 7 5 2
                    ♡ 5
                    ♢ A K 4 2
                    ♣ 3
♠ K 10 6 3                                    ♠ Q
♡ 4 2                                         ♡ 9 7 6
♢ Q 8 3                                       ♢ J 9 5
♣ J 10 9 5                                    ♣ K 8 7 6 4 2
                    ♠ 4
                    ♡ A K Q J 10 8 3
                    ♢ 10 7 6
                    ♣ A Q
```

Don't ask me how or why, but South landed in a 7♡ contract that appears to hinge on bringing home dummy's spades for a discard or two.

A red-suit lead might have scuttled the slam early, but mercifully West had been dealt a club sequence and led the top of it. West's ♣J rode to South's ♣Q.

Now that South had no need to ruff his ♣Q, he confidently drew trumps in three rounds, discarding diamonds from dummy.

Then he set about ruffing out the spades: ♠4 to dummy's ♠A, felling East's ♠Q, low spade from dummy—oops, East's black card is a club, not a spade. Now South can finish ruffing out the spades using dummy's two diamond entries, but lacks a third dummy entry to cash any.

How did the declarer in the other room find the extra entry to take all 13 tricks in a heart contract after the same opening lead?

The other South started spades immediately after winning the ♣Q at Trick 1. When East discarded a club on the second spade at Trick 3, South ruffed dummy's ♠2.

He found the extra dummy entry by ruffing his ♣A with dummy's lone trump. From there, the road home was swift and clear.

DEAL 7. FORCING AN ENTRY

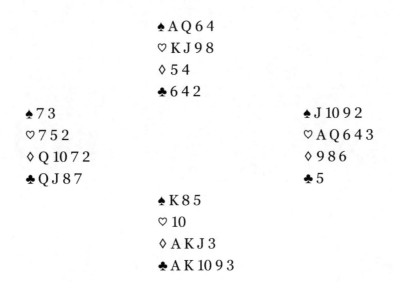

♠ A Q 6 4
♥ K J 9 8
♦ 5 4
♣ 6 4 2

♠ 7 3   ♠ J 10 9 2
♥ 7 5 2   ♥ A Q 6 4 3
♦ Q 10 7 2   ♦ 9 8 6
♣ Q J 8 7   ♣ 5

♠ K 8 5
♥ 10
♦ A K J 3
♣ A K 10 9 3

After a 2♦ "reverse" and a 3♣ preference, South placed the contract in 3NT and received an opening lead in the unbid suit, the ♠7. Counting seven top tricks with prospects for more everywhere, declarer won in hand and attacked the suit with the most cards first.

He cashed the ♣A and continued with the ♣10, the right card to cater to a possible ♣QJxx with East. Unfortunately, it was West who held ♣QJxx. After winning the ♣J, West persisted in spades, dislodging one of dummy's scarce entries.

Oops, only one long-suit winner available in clubs. When nothing good happened in any suit to let declarer set up a ninth trick, 3NT was doomed.

Where was the elusive ninth trick?

It was there if you looked in the right places. In the other room, declarer looked not at the longest suit, but at the suit with the most *establishable* (as distinguished from *top* or *total*) tricks.

At Trick 2, right after winning the ♠K, South attacked hearts. She overtook her ♥10 with dummy's ♥J to ensure an eventual two heart tricks while dummy had the two vital spade entries to establish and cash them.

DEAL 8. REACHING DUMMY

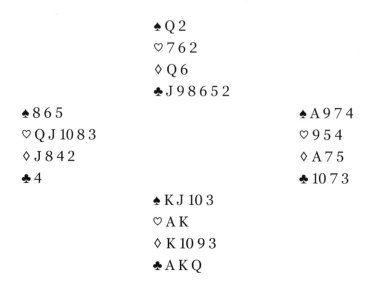

```
                      ♠ Q 2
                      ♡ 7 6 2
                      ◊ Q 6
                      ♣ J 9 8 6 5 2
   ♠ 8 6 5                            ♠ A 9 7 4
   ♡ Q J 10 8 3                       ♡ 9 5 4
   ◊ J 8 4 2                          ◊ A 7 5
   ♣ 4                               ♣ 10 7 3
                      ♠ K J 10 3
                      ♡ A K
                      ◊ K 10 9 3
                      ♣ A K Q
```

After a routine auction to 3NT, declarer won the opening ♡Q lead and unblocked his three top clubs. He wondered how to reach dummy to cash three more clubs while setting up a ninth trick somewhere … before the defenders could dislodge his remaining heart stopper and run hearts.

South tried leading low to dummy's ♠Q, but it fell to East's ♠A. East's heart return left declarer helpless to take more than eight tricks before the defenders could take the five they needed to beat 3NT.

Just unlucky, or did he miss a better play for nine tricks?

In the other room, declarer counted his tricks. Six clubs, two hearts and one spade or diamond would come to nine, the high road. So would three clubs, two hearts, three spades and one diamond, the low road.

A little third-grade arithmetic convinced declarer that 9 = 9. Not caring which nine tricks he scored, South led the ◊K to Trick 5.

What could East do? If East captured the ◊K with his ◊A, that would open the high road, so he ducked. Only then did South lead low to dummy's ♠Q. East had to win the ♠A, of course, to keep dummy off lead, but South won the heart return and reached Loch Lomond by the low road.

DEAL 9. PLAY IT AGAIN, SAM: NINE EQUALS NINE

```
                      ♠ 3 2
                      ♡ 8 4 2
                      ◊ J 9 7 5 4 2
                      ♣ Q 5
        ♠ A 8 4                          ♠ 10 9 6 5
        ♡ Q 10 7 5 3                     ♡ J 9 6
        ◊ 8                              ◊ 10 6 3
        ♣ 10 9 6 4                       ♣ K 8 7
                      ♠ K Q J 7
                      ♡ A K
                      ◊ A K Q
                      ♣ A J 3 2
```

Was your 23-HCP hand not good enough for you to make 3NT on the previous deal? All right, this time you have 27 HCP. Why are we so good to you?

As before, you reach 3NT with ease and receive a ♡5 opening lead. This time it's diamonds that you unblock before leading to Trick 5, and you have only one possible entry to dummy, not two. The rest of the diamonds will give you the nine tricks you need.

South saw dummy's ♣Q as a possible dummy entry and led low towards her. Not good enough. East won the ♣K and continued hearts. When West won the ♠A, he cashed three heart tricks. Down one.

Was there a road to nine tricks?

This time, we hope, you saw it. As before, it doesn't matter which nine tricks you take.

In the other room, after unblocking diamonds, declarer led the ♣J, East had no winning option.

If he won the ♣K, dummy's ♣Q would become an entry to dummy's diamonds.

If he ducked, declarer could drive out the ♠A to set up two spades and get nine tricks the other way: two spades, two hearts, three diamonds, and two clubs. Nine is still nine.

DEAL 10. SEARCHING FOR A TRICK AND AN ENTRY

```
                        ♠ Q 8 4
                        ♡ Q 10 5 3
                        ◊ 8 5 4
                        ♣ 7 6 4
        ♠ J 10 7                           ♠ 2
        ♡ J 8 7                            ♡ K 9 6 4
        ◊ Q                                ◊ K J 10 9 7 6 3
        ♣ K Q J 10 5 3                     ♣ 9
                        ♠ A K 9 6 5 3
                        ♡ A 2
                        ◊ A 2
                        ♣ A 8 2
```

After South opened 1♠, West's 3♣ Weak Jump Overcall shut out East, who could not bid 3◊ because it would be forcing, but it did not shut out South. South had an easy 3♠ rebid; North raised bravely to 4♠.

West led the ♣K. South won the ♣A and saw four apparent losers. He hoped eventually to establish a heart trick to discard one of them. He drew trumps in three rounds. Then he cashed the ♡A and led the ♡2.

No way home from here. Even after guessing correctly to insert dummy's ♡10, he had no entry to use the ♡Q. Down one.

How would *you* have used your limited assets?

By conserving them, we hope. In the other room, South saw one dummy entry, the ♠Q. He won the opening lead and cashed only his ♠AK. Leaving the last trump outstanding, he led the ♡A and continued with the ♡2. When West followed low, South guessed well to insert dummy's ♡10.

East won the ♡K, but South won his ◊J shift and led to dummy's ♠Q. This not only drew West's last trump but provided the entry he needed to cash dummy's ♡Q for a tenth trick. Making 4♠.

DEAL 11. ONE MORE DUMMY ENTRY, PLEASE

```
                      ♠ Q 5
                      ♡ 7 6 4 3
                      ◊ A 5 3 2
                      ♣ J 4 3
        ♠ 10 9 8 7 4 2                      ♠ 6 3
        ♡ A Q 9                             ♡ 10 8 5 2
        ◊ 9 7                               ◊ Q 10 8
        ♣ A 7                               ♣ Q 6 5 2
                      ♠ A K J
                      ♡ K J
                      ◊ K J 6 4
                      ♣ K 10 9 8
```

South opened 1◊ and reached 3NT after West competed in spades. Being unable to seek a heart trick safely, South knew he would need to catch East with the minor-suit queens to come to nine tricks.

After winning Trick 1 with dummy's ♠Q, he started clubs by letting dummy's ♣J ride to West's ♣A. West exited in spades; after winning the ♠A, declarer led low to dummy's ◊A to finesse against the ◊Q, which fell beneath his ◊K on the third round.

South's ◊6 and ♣K provided his sixth and seventh tricks, and he still had the ♠K for his eighth. But West held three hearts including the ♡A and ♡Q behind him. South had to lose three heart tricks after East won the ♣Q and shifted to hearts.

Could you have found your way back to the dummy to repeat your successful finesse against East's ♣Q?

Not if you squandered your ◊4 when you led "low" to dummy's ◊A. You needed to keep it to use dummy's ◊5 as a fourth-round entry.

Little things mean a lot in bridge. The smallest slips can come back to haunt you in the strangest ways.

Were you paying attention when we said "declarer led *low*" to dummy's ◊A. Tricky of us! Don't say "low" when you need to specify the ◊6.

In the other room, South made 3NT by leading the ◊6 to dummy's ◊A. Starting clubs with dummy's ♣3 might also have eased declarer's path, but the play of the diamond spot-cards was crucial.

DEAL 12. A QUICK TWO-STEP QUIZ

♠ 9 8 5
♡ 5 4
◊ K J 10 9 8 3
♣ Q 10

♠ A Q 3 2
♡ A 9 8 6 3
◊ Q
♣ A K 8

Partner opens a Weak 2◊ Bid as dealer on favorable vulnerability, and you respond 3NT forthwith. West leads the ♣6, you play the ♣10 from dummy, and East follows with the ♣4.

(1) Which card do you play from your hand at Trick 1?

(2) Which cards do you play from both hands, dummy's as well as your own, at Trick 2?

You had two tests to pass.

At Trick 1, dummy's ♣10 could have held the trick, but you had to overtake with the ♣K to preserve the ♣8 as an entry to dummy's ♣Q.

At Trick 2, you had to overtake your ◊Q with dummy's ◊K to keep playing diamonds to drive out the ◊A.

Did you pass both tests?

DEAL 13. NEED AN ENTRY? MAKE AN OFFER

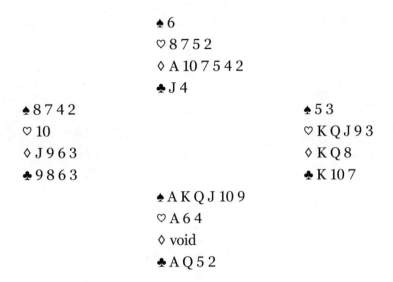

```
                          ♠ 6
                          ♡ 8 7 5 2
                          ◊ A 10 7 5 4 2
                          ♣ J 4
        ♠ 8 7 4 2                          ♠ 5 3
        ♡ 10                               ♡ K Q J 9 3
        ◊ J 9 6 3                          ◊ K Q 8
        ♣ 9 8 6 3                          ♣ K 10 7
                          ♠ A K Q J 10 9
                          ♡ A 6 4
                          ◊ void
                          ♣ A Q 5 2
```

After East opened 1♡ as dealer, South drove to game in spades. East overtook West's ♡10 opening lead with the ♡J and South won the ♡A.

Needing to reach dummy to score the ◊A for a tenth trick, he tried leading the ♣2 to dummy's ♣J. East won the ♣K and cashed two heart winners, then switched to the ♠3.

Declarer lost the last trick to West's ♣9. Down one.

Was there a way to reach dummy and score the ◊A for his tenth trick?

Yes, by making East an offer that he could not refuse. Danny learned that from Uncle Walter, but don't tell anyone.

In the other room, declarer led the ♣Q to Trick 2. Mama Mia, what could poor East do?

If East ducked, South could cash the ♣A next, ruff the ♣2 in dummy, and cash dummy's ◊A to make an overtrick. So East won the ♣K, cashed two high hearts on which West discarded diamonds, and led another high heart.

Declarer ruffed, drew trumps, crossed to dummy's ♣J, and threw his remaining low club on dummy's ◊A ... finally.

DEAL 14. AN EXTRA ENTRY FOR THE SECOND SUIT

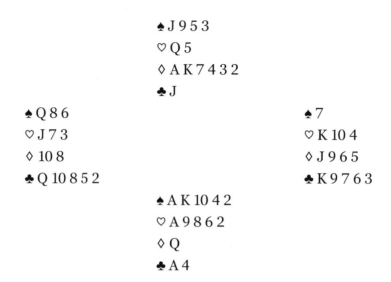

```
                    ♠ J 9 5 3
                    ♡ Q 5
                    ◊ A K 7 4 3 2
                    ♣ J
  ♠ Q 8 6                              ♠ 7
  ♡ J 7 3                              ♡ K 10 4
  ◊ 10 8                               ◊ J 9 6 5
  ♣ Q 10 8 5 2                         ♣ K 9 7 6 3
                    ♠ A K 10 4 2
                    ♡ A 9 8 6 2
                    ◊ Q
                    ♣ A 4
```

North and South bid briskly to 6♠. West led the ♣5. South captured East's ♣K with the ♣A. Noting that a 2-2 trump split would see him home with a likely overtrick (Plan A), South cashed the ♠A and ♠K.

When East discarded a club on the second spade, declarer switched to Plan B: setting up diamonds: ◊Q, club ruff in dummy, ◊A, ◊K ... oops, West ruffed with the master trump and exited in clubs.

The ruff-and-sluff did South no good. He had only one dummy entry but needed two. He needed to ruff out East's diamond stopper and return to dummy to cash the rest of the diamonds. Down one.

Can you devise a "Plan C" that would cover all bases?

Setting up diamonds is best, but may require an extra dummy entry.
In the other room, South cashed the ◊Q at Trick 2. Then he cashed the ♠A and led the ♠2. West won the ♠Q and tapped dummy with a club.

However, South ruffed a diamond high, entered dummy with the ♠J to draw West's last trump. He ran dummy's diamonds from the top to discard four low hearts and take the rest.
Using dummy's ♠J as an extra entry did the job.

DEAL 15. NEED AN EXTRA ENTRY? RUFF A WINNER

```
                    ♠ J 8 2
                    ♡ 4
                    ◊ A 10 9 7 6
                    ♣ A 8 6 5
    ♠ K 6                            ♠ 5
    ♡ Q J 9 2                        ♡ 10 8 7 5 3
    ◊ J 5 2                          ◊ K Q 8 4
    ♣ K J 9 2                        ♣ Q 7 4
                    ♠ A Q 10 9 7 4 3
                    ♡ A K 6
                    ◊ 3
                    ♣ 10 3
```

North and South reached a seemingly thin 6♠ based on loads of trumps, excellent controls and good shape. If declarer lost a trick to the ♠K, he might have to lose a club trick also. Fortunately, West led a safe ♡Q.

South won with the ♡A, ruffed his low heart in dummy, and relied on a spade finesse to come to 12 tricks. When he lost to West's doubleton ♠K, he was left with an unshakeable club loser and went down.

South put all his eggs in the spade basket. Could he have done better?

In the other room, South reached 6♠ also but tried to combine his chances. At Trick 2, he cashed the ♠A hoping the ♠K might fall singleton, a 26% chance. On a good day, it would, but not today.

So he set about trying to ruff out the diamonds in order to discard his low club: ◊A, diamond ruff, heart ruff in dummy, another diamond ruff, and the ♡K *ruffing in dummy*. A third diamond ruff brought down East's last diamond honor. West could overruff or not, but dummy's ♣A provided the entry declarer needed to pitch his low club on dummy's fifth diamond.

By the way, West could have beaten 6♠ by leading clubs. Some of Jim's old friends had a rule: *Lead clubs against slams*. Some Neanderthals swear by it. However, on this deal and many others, when dummy has a long suit, attacking dummy's outside entries early works miracles.

DEAL 16. TIMING THE PLAY TO
UTILIZE A DUMMY ENTRY

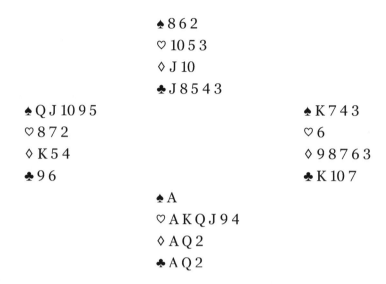

♠ 8 6 2
♡ 10 5 3
◊ J 10
♣ J 8 5 4 3

♠ Q J 10 9 5
♡ 8 7 2
◊ K 5 4
♣ 9 6

♠ K 7 4 3
♡ 6
◊ 9 8 7 6 3
♣ K 10 7

♠ A
♡ A K Q J 9 4
◊ A Q 2
♣ A Q 2

Don't ask us how South guessed to bid this precarious 6♡ slam, or we'll spend sleepless nights dreaming up Wormwood: a convention to locate a guarded ten of trumps in conjunction with jack-fifth in whichever side suit partner favors. For us Neanderthals that's clubs, of course.

West led the ♠Q. As North spread the dummy he fingered the ◊J and said, "Gravy!" "You mean 'pinochle,'" chirped East.

Declarer saw that he needed to set up clubs to get his 12 tricks without risking a diamond finesse. So he won the ♠A and cashed only two top trumps, preserving dummy's precious ♡10 entry.

Then he attacked clubs, cashing the ♣A and leading the ♣Q to offer to whichever defender owned the ♣K. Oops! East won and led his last club for West to ruff. Down one.

How could declarer untangle these tricks and reach the dummy to cash dummy's long clubs while minimizing the danger of a club ruff?

With better timing. In the other room, South avoided letting the defender with the ♣K take it at a time he could give his partner a ruff.

After drawing two rounds of trumps, South led the ♣Q without releasing the ♣A. East could win the ♣K on the first round or the third, but not on the fatal second, when his partner was poised to ruff the next club.

DEAL 17. TAKING NINE TRICKS
WITH LIMITED ENTRIES

```
                        ♠ 5 3
                        ♡ J 7 4
                        ◊ Q 8 2
                        ♣ K 9 8 4 2
    ♠ J 10 9 8                          ♠ 7 6 4 2
    ♡ K 9 5                             ♡ A 10 8
    ◊ 9 6 4                             ◊ 10 7 3
    ♣ 6 5 3                             ♣ A J 7
                        ♠ A K Q
                        ♡ Q 6 3 2
                        ◊ A K J 5
                        ♣ Q 10
```

North raised South's 2NT opening to 3NT. West led the obvious ♠J. Declarer counted seven top tricks in spades and diamonds, and could set up one club. Hearts were too dangerous to tackle for a ninth trick.

So after winning the first spade South sought a second club trick by leading the queen, which held. When he led the ♣10 next, East won the ♣J and returned a spade. Needing two dummy entries to establish and take even one more club trick, but having only one, declarer remained one trick short and went down.

With only one outside entry to dummy, can you ensure two club tricks?

Remember Uncle Walter's advice? Make the defender with the ♣J an offer he can't refuse. So as South did in the other room, lead the ♣10 to Trick 2, and let it ride whether covered or not.

What can East do?

If East lets the ♣10 hold, South continues with the ♣Q and East must duck again to prevent overtricks. Nine tricks!

If East wins the ♣J, upon regaining the lead South overtakes the ♣Q with dummy's ♣K to drive out the ♣A while dummy remains with the ◊Q as an entry. Now East can do no better than shift to hearts to stop overtricks.

DEAL 18. TIME THOSE DUMMY ENTRIES CAREFULLY

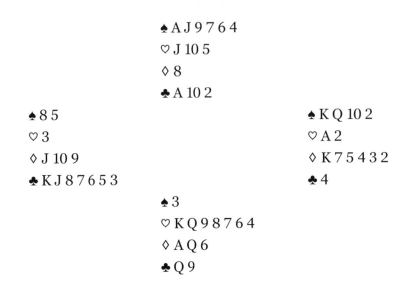

♠ A J 9 7 6 4
♥ J 10 5
♦ 8
♣ A 10 2

♠ 8 5
♥ 3
♦ J 10 9
♣ K J 8 7 6 5 3

♠ K Q 10 2
♥ A 2
♦ K 7 5 4 3 2
♣ 4

♠ 3
♥ K Q 9 8 7 6 4
♦ A Q 6
♣ Q 9

West's "favorable vulnerability" 3♣ opening as dealer had the perverse effect of goading his opponents into bidding an iffy 6♡ they might not have reached had he passed. Fortunately for him, he had a safe ◇J opening lead; a Neanderthal club lead would have been fatal to the defense immediately.

Anyone for a trump lead (the winning lead on this deal)?

We don't think so.

After winning Trick 1, declarer couldn't resist one round of trumps just to feel safe. East won the ♡A and returned his lone club to dislodge dummy's ♣A.

Only then did declarer start spades: ♠A and a spade ruff. Declarer had two trump entries, a trump honor and a diamond ruff, to ruff out the spades but lacked a third entry to dummy to discard his club loser on a long spade. Down one.

Could you have set up *and run* the spades?

Yes, had you begun promptly at Trick 2. No need to worry about overruffs with such good trump spot-cards. ♠A, spade ruff, heart to East's ♡A, and a club shift to drive out dummy's ♣A.

Another spade ruff, heart to dummy's ♡10 drawing the defenders' last trump, and a third spade ruff. Now a diamond ruff puts dummy in to run the established spades.

"You gotta have timing, tick-a-tick-a-tock timing!"

DEAL 19. FORGE AN ENTRY TO DUMMY FIRST

```
                    ♠ A K 8 7 6 5 4
                    ♡ 8 7
                    ◇ 9 4
                    ♣ J 4
    ♠ Q 9                             ♠ J 10 3 2
    ♡ 9 3                             ♡ A 10
    ◇ 10 8 3 2                        ◇ K Q J 6
    ♣ 10 7 6 5 3                      ♣ K 8 2
                    ♠ void
                    ♡ K Q J 6 5 4 2
                    ◇ A 7 5
                    ♣ A Q 9
```

After East opened 1◇ as dealer, South did well to preempt with 4♡ before the opponents could find their spade fit and reach 4♠ as a good save if not a make. No way he could know that it was North who had the long strong spades.

West led the ◇2 to East's ◇J. Uh-oh, four losers! Hoping to win the diamond continuation and ruff a diamond to reach dummy and discard on the top spades, South ducked. East foiled South's plan by cashing the ♡A and continuing the ♡10. Bereft of dummy entries, declarer had to lose a club and another diamond. Down one.

Was there a way to use dummy's assets?

In the other room, the bidding and opening lead were the same, but declarer did not give East a chance to find the killing defense. He won the ◇A at Trick 1 and led the ♣Q immediately. Now East had no winning option.

Capturing the ♣Q with the ♣K would turn dummy's ♣J into an entry for the top spades; ducking would let declarer continue with the ♣A and a club ruff to reach dummy.

"Well done," said North. "You did well not to start with a double, or I'd still be bidding spades."

DEAL 20. LOCKSMITH

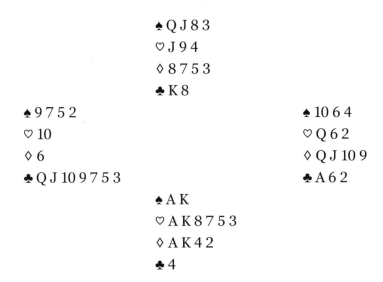

♠ Q J 8 3
♡ J 9 4
◇ 8 7 5 3
♣ K 8

♠ 9 7 5 2
♡ 10
◇ 6
♣ Q J 10 9 7 5 3

♠ 10 6 4
♡ Q 6 2
◇ Q J 10 9
♣ A 6 2

♠ A K
♡ A K 8 7 5 3
◇ A K 4 2
♣ 4

After South opened an Omnibus 2♣ (strong, artificial and forcing), vigorous competition by the opponents in clubs pushed him up to 5♡.

Declarer let West's ♣Q lead hold Trick 1, ruffed East's ♣A at Trick 2, and led the ♡A next. When West's ♡10 fell, South hoped his ♡Q would fall next. South prepared to apologize to North for missing slam as he banged down the ♡K. However, he wasn't in slam and the ♡Q didn't fall.

"Sorry, partner," said South. "Looks like down one. I should have doubled five clubs."

"Down two," said East, showing declarer his diamonds.

"How about just making five hearts?" asked North rhetorically.

How could declarer have done better?

In the other room, pushed to the same contract, South took the fall of the ♡10 at Trick 3 as both a warning that it might be singleton and a beacon shining light on the safe harbor for the contract.

Now dummy's remaining ♡J9 offered a sure entry, so he cashed the ♠AK, not caring if a defender ruffed. Then he led the ♡3 to give the defenders the ♡Q and take the rest.

"I knew I had a fine dummy for you," said North, chalking up plus 650.

DEAL 21. BOTTLE OF WINE
(IN HONOR OF CYMA ARONOW)

```
                    ♠ Q 10 8 6
                    ♡ K 4 3
                    ◇ 7 5 4 2
                    ♣ J 7
     ♠ 5                                ♠ K 4 3
     ♡ Q J 10 7 5                       ♡ A 9 2
     ◇ 9 3                              ◇ K 10 6
     ♣ 10 8 5 3 2                       ♣ K 9 6 4
                    ♠ A J 9 7 2
                    ♡ 8 6
                    ◇ A Q J 8
                    ♣ A Q
```

The local bridge club's Christmas Party featured a Swiss Teams, and the hostess offered a bottle of Pinot Grand Fenwick as a prize to the last player to win a trick with a deuce—provided it was the right play (no ruffing partner's ace for the wine). On the last deal of the last match, East opened 1♣ as dealer, and North's raise of South's hefty 1♠ overcall propelled the pair to 4♠.

West led the top of his heart sequence and continued hearts until South ruffed with the ♠2. South raised his arm to call the director and demand his bottle, but North waved him off, pointing to his own ◇2: "You could at least wait until Trick 13."

South cashed the ♠A but the ♠K didn't fall. East won the next spade and led his third spade for safe exit.

Winning in dummy, declarer finessed diamonds successfully, then cashed the ◇A. When East's ◇K didn't fall, the best South could do was throw him in with it to force a club return, endplay for down one.

The director ruled *NO WINE*. Why?

The declarer in the other room faced the same problem, but he ruffed the third heart with the ♠A. Then when he fed East the ♠K, he had *three* spade entries to dummy. He was able to finesse twice in diamonds and once in clubs.

Making 4♠, but still no bottle of wine.

DEAL 22. CREATE AN ENTRY TO DUMMY

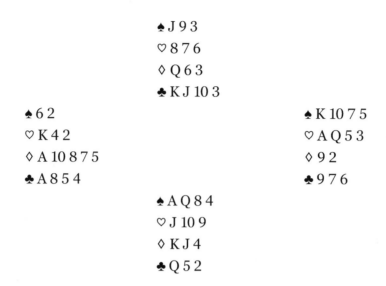

```
                      ♠ J 9 3
                      ♡ 8 7 6
                      ◊ Q 6 3
                      ♣ K J 10 3
   ♠ 6 2                              ♠ K 10 7 5
   ♡ K 4 2                            ♡ A Q 5 3
   ◊ A 10 8 7 5                       ◊ 9 2
   ♣ A 8 5 4                          ♣ 9 7 6
                      ♠ A Q 8 4
                      ♡ J 10 9
                      ◊ K J 4
                      ♣ Q 5 2
```

South's weak notrump as dealer bought the contract and fetched the beer card (to any teetotaler who may read this, the ◊7) from East on opening lead. Declarer captured East's ◊9 ("the Curse of Scotland") with the ◊J and started clubs.

West ducked twice and won the third club as East followed low, higher, highest to suggest a heart shift. West duly switched to the ♡2, and East won with the *queen*. East's ◊2 return posed an insoluble dilemma to South. Ducking would let West win the ◊A and put declarer back in his hand; rising with the ◊K would let West duck to keep dummy off lead.

Down two either way, as declarer could neither cash dummy's fourth club nor finesse in spades for his contract.

Hard headache, easy solution. Do you see it?

Mike Lawrence says some of the most innocent plays in bridge can come back to haunt you in the strangest of ways.

In the other room, declarer won Trick 1 with the ◊K, not the ◊J. Now dummy's ◊Q became an entry, and declarer romped home with two spades, two diamonds, and three clubs.

"You jack of diamonds, oh you jack of diamonds, you robba my pocket of silver and gold." Or maybe only two tricks.

DEAL 23. "NO TRICK SHALL BE CASHED BEFORE ITS TIME"

```
                 ♠ A 5 4 3
                 ♡ J 7 6 4
                 ♦ 10 4 3
                 ♣ K Q
   ♠ K 10 8 2                    ♠ Q 9 6
   ♡ Q 10 8                      ♡ K 9 3 2
   ♦ J 8 6                       ♦ A 9 7
   ♣ J 6 3                       ♣ 8 7 4
                 ♠ J 7
                 ♡ A 5
                 ♦ K Q 5 2
                 ♣ A 10 9 5 2
```

Should South open 1♣ or 1♦ with this hand? Depending on which of us you ask, and on which day of the week, you may get different answers.

Fibonacci's Law says that the two cards just below an honor are virtually as good as the honor itself to bolster another honor in the suit. Who's Fibonacci? One theory says he's a little old winegrower in Tuscany.

At any rate, South opened a 15-to-17 HCP 1NT, just as he would with ♣AJ532 instead of his actual club holding, and reached 3NT via Stayman.

All other leads looking worse, West led the ♠2, ducked to East's ♠Q. East returned the ♠9 to West's ♠K and dummy's ♠A.

Eager to run clubs, declarer unblocked dummy's two honors, and led dummy's ♦3 to his ♦K, which held.

Good news: the clubs ran. Bad news: Declarer could only take eight tricks. He led the ♦2, hoping the ♦A was now singleton. Down one.

A poor contract, but could it be made?

In the other room, South reached 3NT by the same route. Play started similarly, but declarer started diamonds from dummy at Trick 3. Only after winning the ♦K did he unblock dummy's club monarchs and lead another diamond towards his ♦Q.

East could win and lead his last spade to hold declarer to contract, but South had his nine tricks.

DEAL 24. UNBLOCK TO CREATE AN ENTRY TO DUMMY

Frank Stewart always has wonderful deals in his daily newspaper column. Here is one from a few years ago of which Frank wrote, "Requires a degree of perfection that not many declarers could produce."

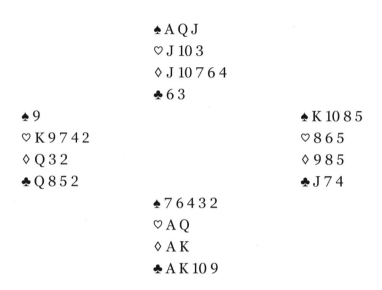

West led the ♡4 against South's 3NT. South won the ♡Q and saw that eight tricks looked easy: two in each suit if the spade finesse lost, and a ninth if it won. So he tried that finesse, thinking he could look for a ninth trick somewhere if it failed.

East won the ♠K and returned a heart to declarer's ♡A. South cashed his two top diamonds; the ◊Q did not fall. Two more spades and two top clubs left him one trick short, and the defenders ran hearts to beat him.

What line of play did Frank suggest?

Win the ♡Q, unblock both top diamonds and cross to dummy's ♠A. Then discard the ♡A on dummy's ◊J. A defender will win the ◊Q but then declarer can force an entry to dummy in spades if the defenders don't put dummy in with a heart trick.

Now declarer has four diamond tricks and two top clubs available, and one trick already home in each major. He cannot be prevented from reaching dummy with a second trick in one major or the other for a ninth trick. The defenders will have to be careful to avoid giving declarer a tenth.

Thank you, Frank.

DEAL 25. NO CHEAP TRICKS!

```
                    ♠ Q 8 6
                    ♡ 5
                    ◊ K Q 10 7 5 4
                    ♣ 10 7 2
     ♠ K 9 7 4 2                        ♠ 5 3
     ♡ K 9 8 7                          ♡ J 10 4
     ◊ 3                                ◊ J 9 8 2
     ♣ K 9 3                            ♣ Q 8 5 4
                    ♠ A J 10
                    ♡ A Q 6 3 2
                    ◊ A 6
                    ♣ A J 6
```

West led a fourth-highest ♠4 against South's 3NT. Silently thanking West for the supposed gift of a trick, South remembered what his rubber-bridge-playing girlfriend taught him before she ran off with a used-car salesman: "It's overtricks that buys Cadillacs."

South won the ♠10 and played diamonds from the top. Oops, when West showed out on the second diamond, dummy was dead.

Declarer flailed away, discarding a heart, leading to the ♠A and throwing West in with a third spade, but West cashed two more spades. In the five-card ending declarer remained with ♡AQ and ♣AJx and had to lose two more tricks when West exited with the ♣K.

North said, "I thought you had nine easy tricks. What happened?"

Do you see what happened?

As Mike Lawrence says, having and taking are not the same. 3NT was at risk only if a defender had jack-fourth in diamonds, and that hurdle could be surmounted if declarer retained a dummy entry.

In the other room, South foresaw the danger. Reading West for the ♠K, he won Trick 1 with the ♠A, played four rounds of diamonds discarding hearts and losing to East's ◊J. He won East's heart shift with the ♡A and reached dummy with the ♠Q. Nine tricks guaranteed.

DEAL 26. WHO'S CLUMSIER THAN WHOM?

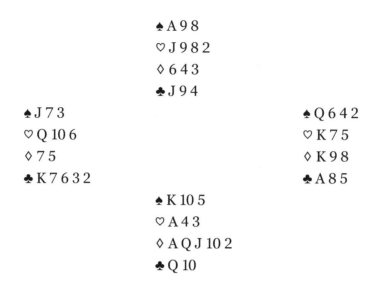

```
                    ♠ A 9 8
                    ♡ J 9 8 2
                    ◊ 6 4 3
                    ♣ J 9 4
    ♠ J 7 3                        ♠ Q 6 4 2
    ♡ Q 10 6                       ♡ K 7 5
    ◊ 7 5                          ◊ K 9 8
    ♣ K 7 6 3 2                    ♣ A 8 5
                    ♠ K 10 5
                    ♡ A 4 3
                    ◊ A Q J 10 2
                    ♣ Q 10
```

Hang around bridge clubs long enough and you'll see amazingly improbable things. South was inept at arithmetic and probably miscounted his points. He opened 2NT. North's raise to 3NT ended the auction.

West led a normal ♣3. Declarer played the ♣4 from dummy and followed with the ♣10 when East won the ♣A. East returned the ♣8 and West, reading South for ♣Q10 doubleton, ducked South's ♣Q.

South crossed to dummy's ♠A and finessed diamonds successfully. Lacking another dummy entry, he cashed the ◊A and prayed the ◊K would fall. When it didn't, 3NT was doomed.

How did declarer go wrong?

By failing to unblock the ♣Q at Trick 1. Had he done so, dummy's ♣J would have supplied an extra dummy entry.

In the other room South pulled the 2NT card from her bidding box and didn't realize it until after North raised to 3NT. Did she make 3NT?

No. There, reading West for at most 4 HCP, East played the ♣8 to Trick 1. Curtains!

DEAL 27. THE SHORT HAND'S PLAYS
FROM VIRTUAL EQUALS

"Good heavens, does everybody overbid? Now they're bidding it on 24!" said the curmudgeon, referring to 3NT and high-card points.

```
                    ♠ Q 10 9 8
                    ♡ 5 3 2
                    ◊ J 9 7
                    ♣ J 10 9
    ♠ A 3 2                         ♠ K 6 4
    ♡ 9 8 6                         ♡ 10 7 4
    ◊ 6 5                           ◊ K 8 4 3
    ♣ Q 7 5 3 2                     ♣ A 8 6
                    ♠ J 7 5
                    ♡ A K Q J
                    ◊ A Q 10 2
                    ♣ K 4
```

North raised South's not-quite robust 2NT opening to 3NT. West led the ♣3 and South raised an eyebrow.

West led the ♣3. Declarer started well, unblocking the ♣K under East's ♣A to assure a dummy entry if the defenders persisted in clubs. West won East's ♣8 return with the ♣Q and cleared the suit. Needing eight tricks in the red suits, declarer let dummy's ◊J ride.

"Doesn't anyone believe in Mother Goose any more?" asked declarer when it held. "Always cover an honor with an honor." When he continued with dummy's ◊9, East still declined to cover, but when West showed out on the ◊A next, 3NT was doomed.

North said, "Partner, after making the hard play, how could you miss the easy one?" What did North mean by that?

In the other room, South made the easy play. With kangaroo sequences in both hands, he began his finessing by leading the lowest card from dummy that he could safely underplay, the ◊9. That let him lead the higher ◊J next and underplay again on the second round.

DEAL 28. TRADE ONE FOR THREE TO
CREATE A DUMMY ENTRY

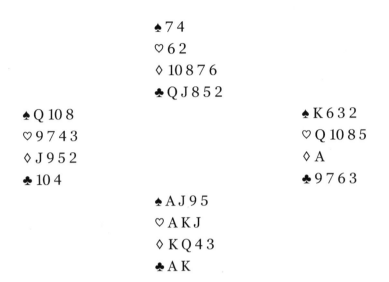

♠ 7 4
♡ 6 2
◊ 10 8 7 6
♣ Q J 8 5 2

♠ Q 10 8
♡ 9 7 4 3
◊ J 9 5 2
♣ 10 4

♠ K 6 3 2
♡ Q 10 8 5
◊ A
♣ 9 7 6 3

♠ A J 9 5
♡ A K J
◊ K Q 4 3
♣ A K

South drove to 3NT all on his own. West led a seemingly friendly ◊2. East won the ◊A, as declarer played low from both hands, and made an attractive heart shift. The dear opponents had given South tricks he might not have garnered on his own: a second diamond and a third heart.

Now South could count eight winners. He unblocked his top clubs, but when (surprise?) the ◊J did not fall under his ◊K and ◊Q, he eventually lost two spades, one heart and another diamond. Down one.

By now we're sure you see the correct play. Do you?

South in the other room did. Receiving the same lead against 3NT, he dropped the ◊K under East's ◊A. This East shifted to spades. West captured South's ♠9 with the ♠10 and exited with a sly ◊5, but South overtook dummy's ◊7 with the ◊Q.

Declarer unblocked both clubs and exited in diamonds. The defenders were helpless to shut out dummy's three long clubs.

Would you buy a used Cadillac from that South?

DEAL 29. NO CHEAP TRICKS!

```
                    ♠ 6 4 3
                    ♡ 10 4
                    ◇ K J 10 9 5
Henry               ♣ Q 7 5          Eliza
♠ J 7 5                              ♠ Q 9 8 2
♡ K 6 3                              ♡ J 9 8 5
◇ 8 4                               ◇ A 7 2
♣ K J 8 6 2                          ♣ 9 3
                    ♠ A K 10
                    ♡ A Q 7 2
                    ◇ Q 6 3
                    ♣ A 10 4
```

The sly South, a devout five-card majorite, thought it very clever always to open his poorer minor with flat hands. "They never know to lead it against me!" he confided one day when Danny gave him a lift to a nearby tournament. Sure enough, North raised to 2◇ and South bid 3NT directly.

South could not suppress a grin when an unsuspecting West led the ♣6, which he covered gingerly with dummy's ♣7.

"No cheap tricks," said East as he played the ♣9.

"That's what you think," said South, winning with the ♣10. When he started diamonds, East ducked twice. He returned the ♣3 upon winning the third diamond. No way home from there; South finished down two.

Was there a way home? And what's this about "cheap tricks?"

Yes, there was a way home, as North pointed out in a brief post mortem. "Didn't you count three clubs higher than Henry's six? He could only have led from king-jack-eight. So capture Eliza's nine with your ace, and my fair lady will open the jewel-box for you after you've knocked out the ace of diamonds."

In the other room, South did not believe in cheap tricks. He opened 1♣, his better minor, and jumped to 2NT over North's 1◇ response. North raised to 3NT, happy to have the ♣Q as a likely outside entry.

Forewarned about clubs, West in the other room led the ♡3, and with normal play, declarer racked up ten tricks.

29

DEAL 30. QUEEN'S GAMBIT DECLINED

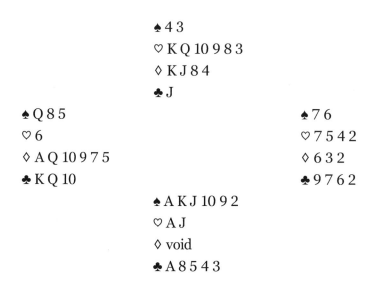

```
                  ♠ 4 3
                  ♡ K Q 10 9 8 3
                  ◊ K J 8 4
                  ♣ J
♠ Q 8 5                           ♠ 7 6
♡ 6                               ♡ 7 5 4 2
◊ A Q 10 9 7 5                    ◊ 6 3 2
♣ K Q 10                          ♣ 9 7 6 2
                  ♠ A K J 10 9 2
                  ♡ A J
                  ◊ void
                  ♣ A 8 5 4 3
```

Despite West's 1◊ opening as dealer, South could not be deterred from driving to 6♠ after North overcalled 1♡. West was too cagy to try to cash the ◊A. He led the ♣K to drive out declarer's ♣A.

Placing all the missing high cards with the opening bidder, South eschewed any finesse against East and cashed both top trumps in hope of dropping a short ♠Q with West. On a good day, the queen's head would roll and declarer could finish trumps, run hearts and make an overtrick, but this was not a good day for overtricks.

Or was it? Can you see how the declarer in the other room made an overtrick?

When Jim posed this question to a small group of bridge players who after the game, Sy the Cynic said, "Sure Jim, I saw your namby-pamby friend Moshe walk into the other room. I'll bet he stopped in four spades."

Well, no, Sy, Moshe was West, and he too led the ♣K against 6♠. Declarer won the ♣A, but she led the ♠9 to Trick 2. Moshe ducked, hoping his partner had a singleton ♠A or doubleton ♠K. Overtrick time!

Jim heard Moshe curse out a dead basketball player: "Elgin, Elgin, how could you do this to me? You told me, 'The trick always comes back.' This time it didn't. If Marshall were alive, he'd sue you for the lost IMP."

DEAL 31. A KING'S RANSOM

      ♠ 7 6
      ♡ 10 4
      ◇ K 9 6 5 3
      ♣ 8 7 4 3

♠ A Q 10 9 5   ♠ J 8 4 2
♡ 8   ♡ Q 9 3
◇ Q J 10 8   ◇ 7 4 2
♣ 10 6 5   ♣ Q J 9

      ♠ K 3
      ♡ A K J 7 6 5 2
      ◇ A
      ♣ A K 2

South reached 4♡ after opening an Omnibus 2♣. He won Trick 1 with the ◇A and cashed both top trumps. The ♡Q didn't fall.

Unable to reach dummy, declarer lost two spades, one club, and one trump. Dummy's ◇K is still waiting to be cashed. Down one.

Do you see how the declarer in the other room ransomed the ◇K?

There West risked a 2♠ overcall. Not a bad idea over an Omnibus 2♣, before the strong hand can strut his stuff!

To force a dummy entry, South led the ♡J to Trick 2. East chose to win the ♡Q, but now dummy's ♡10 was an entry to dummy's ◇K, on which declarer threw his club loser.

DEAL 32. CREATE AN ENTRY TO
IMPROVE YOUR CHANCES

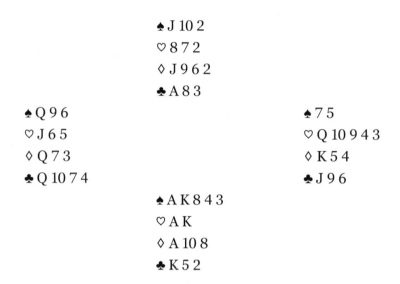

```
              ♠ J 10 2
              ♡ 8 7 2
              ◊ J 9 6 2
              ♣ A 8 3
♠ Q 9 6                         ♠ 7 5
♡ J 6 5                         ♡ Q 10 9 4 3
◊ Q 7 3                         ◊ K 5 4
♣ Q 10 7 4                      ♣ J 9 6
              ♠ A K 8 4 3
              ♡ A K
              ◊ A 10 8
              ♣ K 5 2
```

A misguided "Puppet Stayman" auction led to an inferior 4♠ contract, with possibly two losers in diamonds and one in each black suit. Declarer won the opening club lead in dummy and let the ♠J ride for an immediate trump finesse. It lost to West's ♠Q.

Declarer had too few dummy entries to finesse diamonds twice, so he had to rely on catching East with either both the ◊K and ◊Q, or just one diamond monarch guarded by only one foot soldier.

No such luck. South lost two diamond tricks and to both black queens. Down one.

Can you see the alternative plan that South in the other room tried in the same silly contract, and why it offered much better chances?

West's low-club opening lead offered a clue. The probability that he had both missing diamond honors *and didn't lead the ◊K* was virtually nil. So finessing diamonds twice was virtually 100%.

So in the other room South won the opening club lead in hand and played the ♠A and another, losing to West's ♠Q. He remained with two dummy entries. After finishing trumps in dummy, he was able to finesse diamonds twice and the contract rolled home.

SAVING DUMMY'S ENTRIES

DEAL 33. NO FINESSES, KEEP YOUR ENTRIES INTACT

```
                        ♠ Q 5 3
                        ♡ A 9 4
                        ◊ 10 5 3
                        ♣ 9 7 5 4
        ♠ J 10 9 6                      ♠ 8 4 2
        ♡ Q 8 6 3                      ♡ J 10 5
        ◊ J 6                          ◊ Q 9 7 4
        ♣ Q 8 2                        ♣ A 6 3
                        ♠ A K 7
                        ♡ K 7 2
                        ◊ A K 8 2
                        ♣ K J 10
```

West led the ♠J against South's 3NT. Declarer had seven top tricks and needed two club tricks to make. Declarer won the first trick with dummy's ♠Q and finessed the ♣J. West won the ♣Q and shifted to the ♡3.

Suddenly declarer was in trouble. After capturing East's ♡10, he led the ♣K. East won the ♣A and returned the ♡J. Declarer let it hold and took the next heart with dummy's last entry, the ♡A. With clubs blocked, declarer had two high clubs but no entry to dummy's ♣9. Down one.

How did the declarer in the other room find his way home?

No finesses, thank you. He won the opening lead with his ♠A to preserve an entry to dummy. Then led the ♣K while dummy's entries were still intact. Now declarer was a step ahead.

East won the ♣A and shifted to the ♡J, but declarer was in control. After dislodging West's ♣Q, he had an easy nine tricks.

DEAL 34. FINDING AND MAINTAINING DUMMY ENTRIES

```
                    ♠ 4 2
                    ♡ 6 5 3 2
                    ◇ Q 10 9
                    ♣ 8 5 4 2
     ♠ J 9 8 5                      ♠ K 10 7 3
     ♡ A K Q 9                      ♡ J 8 4
     ◇ 6 5 4                        ◇ K 7 3 2
     ♣ A 7                          ♣ J 3
                    ♠ A Q 6
                    ♡ 10 7
                    ◇ A J 8
                    ♣ K Q 10 9 6
```

After a competitive auction of which no one can be proud, South was pushed to 4♣. West led and continued high hearts. Declarer ruffed low and led the ♣K to West's ♣A. West exited passively in trumps.

Short of dummy entries to finesse, declarer played the ◇A and led the ◇8 to dummy's ◇Q. East won the ◇K and stuck him back in his hand with a third diamond. Down two.

Did dummy have any assets that could have helped declarer home?

Well, yes, he could have saved one trick by leading the ◇J instead of the ◇8 to dummy's ◇Q, but that still gives him only nine tricks.

The declarer in the other room took care to ruff the third heart with the ♣9. Then she was able to lead her precious ♣6 to dummy's ♣8. Another reason the eight of trumps is the most underrated card in bridge!

After leading the ◇Q from dummy, she took care to unblock her ◇J when East played low. Upon repeating the diamond finesse, she remained with a dummy entry to finesse spades successfully for a smooth ten tricks.

DEAL 35. THE DUFFER'S DICTUM

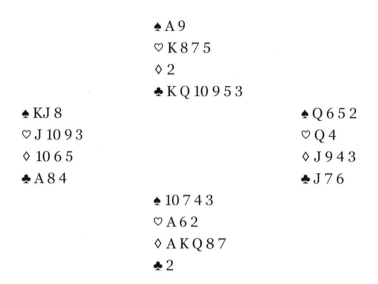

West led the ♡J after South responded 1◊ to North's 1♣, rebid 1♠ over North's 1♡, and jumped to 3NT over North's 2♣.

Eric Kokish, who has an encyclopedic knowledge of bridge, once wrote that Danny has 742 "Laws" in bridge. Danny has lost count, but if Eric is right, here's number 743: "The Duffer's Dictum: Tricks taken in the duffer's hand are worth more than tricks taken in his caddy's hand."

Oops, did Danny say "caddy"? He must have meant *partner*.

South counted two outside entries to dummy's clubs but only one outside entry to his own diamonds. To preserve that entry, he won the heart lead in dummy, then played diamonds from the top.

East won the fourth diamond and returned the ♡Q to South's ♡A. South's fifth diamond was his sixth trick. He led the ♣2. West ducked, so dummy's ♣Q won, but dummy's ♠A was his eighth and last trick. Down one.

Could declarer have made 3NT?

In the other room, South also received the ♡J lead against 3NT, but she counted tricks before entries. She won the ♡A, saving both entries to the suit in which she could *develop more tricks*, clubs. She wound up with four club tricks, one spade trick and two tricks in each red suit. 3NT made.

DEAL 36. TIMING YOUR ENTRIES

```
                    ♠ K Q 6 3
                    ♡ 5 2
                    ◊ 8 7 3
                    ♣ A 8 5 3
    ♠ A 10 7 4                      ♠ J 9 5
    ♡ 10                            ♡ 9 7 6 3
    ◊ A Q 10 2                      ◊ J 6 5 4
    ♣ Q J 10 6                      ♣ 9 7
                    ♠ 8 2
                    ♡ A K Q J 8 4
                    ◊ K 9
                    ♣ K 4 2
```

West's takeout double of South 1♡ opening didn't keep South from reaching 4♡. After winning the ♣Q opening lead with his ♣K, declarer drew trump in four rounds, then started spades.

West ducked the first spade to dummy's ♠K, then South led to his ◊K, hoping to reach his hand promptly for another spade lead. Surprise! The takeout doubler had the ◊A and won it. Then West continued with the ♣10 to drive out dummy's ♣A.

West scored a second diamond, a spade and a club. Down one.

How should declarer have timed the play to use dummy's assets?

The declarer in the other room showed how, by using dummy's trumps for transportation. She won Trick 1 in hand and started spades. After winning dummy's ♠K, she returned to her hand with a trump. Only then did she finish trumps and lead her remaining spade.

West took the ♠A, but dummy's ♣A remained as an entry to the ♠Q, on which declarer discarded her club loser. With 10 tricks assured, she led to her ◊K, losing to West's ◊A as expected but still making 4♡.

DEAL 37. KEEPING AN ENTRY TO DUMMY

After East opened 1♡ in third seat (would you?), South overcalled 1♠. North's 2♣ advance fetched a 2NT rebid from South; North raised to 3NT.

South was pleased to see West lead the ♡J. He resisted the urge to gloat "Got you surrounded!" and covered with dummy's ♡Q, ensuring the first two heart tricks for himself.

"Forgot your Mother Goose?" he asked when East encouraged with the ♡9. East only smiled as South continued, "Always cover an honor with an honor!"

Oops, it was declarer's goose that was cooked by East's good duck. South played on clubs, but East won the second club perforce and exited in spades. With no way back to dummy, declarer fell a trick short, scoring only eight: one club, three spades and two tricks in each red suit.

Do you see another dummy entry?

In the other room, East also chose to open 1♡ (better than 1◊, but we'd sooner *pass*) in third seat. After the same auction and opening lead, South did well to resist her natural urge to cover the ♡J.

Instead she won her ♡A and could not be kept from establishing a heart entry to dummy after driving out the ♣A.

DEAL 38. A TRICK IN TIME SAVES TWO

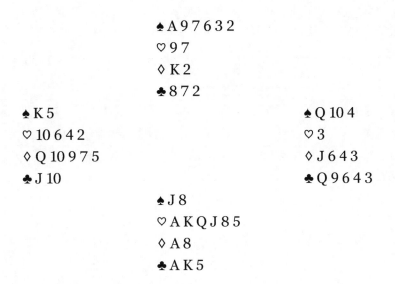

♠A 9 7 6 3 2
♡ 9 7
◊ K 2
♣8 7 2

♠K 5
♡ 10 6 4 2
◊ Q 10 9 7 5
♣J 10

♠Q 10 4
♡ 3
◊ J 6 4 3
♣Q 9 6 4 3

♠J 8
♡ A K Q J 8 5
◊ A 8
♣A K 5

We have something to say about the auction, but this is not the place for it. South drove to a fragile 6♡ and West found a seemingly safe ♣J lead.

Declarer won the ♣A and led the ♠8 to dummy's ♠A before ducking a spade to West's ♠K. The 3-2 spade split was friendly, but with only one entry left in dummy, declarer could not both set up and run spades. Down one.

What basic principle did declarer overlook?

In the other room, South reached the same bad 6♡ slam and received the same deceptively safe ♣J opening lead. South won the ♣A and four top trumps, discarding a club and a spade from dummy. Then he led the ♠J and let West hold the ♠K.

Too late, West shifted to the ◊10. Declarer won the ◊A, led to dummy's ♠A and ruffed a spade to set up the suit. Dummy's ◊K provided the entry needed to run spades and make 6♡.

Note that a diamond lead would have beaten 6♡ by removing a dummy entry in time. When you have four trumps, you'll usually do better to lead from length than shortness.

Oh, that basic principle? Save scarce entries for when you need them the most.

DEAL 39. WRONG SUIT, NO ENTRY

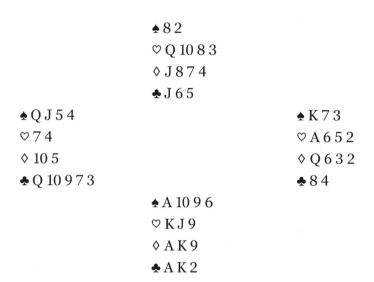

```
                        ♠ 8 2
                        ♡ Q 10 8 3
                        ◊ J 8 7 4
                        ♣ J 6 5
     ♠ Q J 5 4                          ♠ K 7 3
     ♡ 7 4                              ♡ A 6 5 2
     ◊ 10 5                             ◊ Q 6 3 2
     ♣ Q 10 9 7 3                       ♣ 8 4
                        ♠ A 10 9 6
                        ♡ K J 9
                        ◊ A K 9
                        ♣ A K 2
```

After a strong artificial 2♣ opening and 2NT rebid, South's 3♠ reply to Stayman steered West away from a spade opening.

West led the ♣10. When dummy's ♣J won, declarer could count eight tricks merely by driving out the ♡A. He led low to the ♡K and continued with the ♡J. West followed high-low so East knew to duck the second heart.

South led a third heart, and now East won. The club return left South with only eight tricks: three clubs, one spade and two in each red suit. The ♡Q lay stranded on the board with nary an entry to reach it. Down one.

How would you play to take, not just set up, nine tricks?

The declarer in the other room saw a way. Dummy's hearts provided not only tricks but a precious entry. After winning the ♣J and leading to the ♡K, South played on diamonds, hoping for an honor to fall on the first two rounds or a 3-3 split.

When the ◊10 fell on the second top diamond, South led the ◊9. East won the ◊Q and returned his last club. By overtaking his ♡J with dummy's ♡Q, South forced an entry to dummy. Dummy's ◊J provided a third diamond trick to go with three clubs, two hearts and one spade.

Another deal illustrating how 3NT is better when 26 high-card points are divided closer to 13-13 than 23-3. The more evenly the strength is divided, the easier the transportation.

DEAL 40. ASSURING TWELVE TRICKS

```
                    ♠ K 6 5
                    ♡ Q 4 2
                    ◊ K 7 6 5 4
                    ♣ 9 3
   ♠ 10 9                              ♠ Q J 7 4 2
   ♡ A K J 9 6 5                       ♡ 10 8 7 3
   ◊ Q 10 9 3                          ◊ 8
   ♣ 7                                 ♣ 10 6 2
                    ♠ A 8 3
                    ♡ void
                    ◊ A J 2
                    ♣ A K Q J 8 5 4
```

Opposing intervention and preemption in hearts did not keep South from reaching 6♣. South ruffed the ♡K opening lead. Visions of sugar plums danced in his head and he went after a precious 20-point overtrick. An IMP is an IMP, isn't it?

South drew trump, throwing the ♠5 from dummy. Then he crossed to the ◊K and led the ◊4, intending to finesse. When East showed out, South had no way to both set up and cash diamonds. Only 11 tricks: minus 100. "Did you think you were in *seven* clubs?" groaned North.

What was declarer's best play for *six* clubs?

Reaching the same ambitious 6♣ slam in the other room, South remembered she was in 6♣, not 7♣. After ruffing the opening heart lead, she drew trump, discarding a spade from dummy. Then she led the ◊2 and let West's ◊9 hold.

South won West's spade exit with the ♠A and cashed the ◊A. Now dummy's ◊K and a diamond ruff set up dummy's ◊7 for a twelfth trick while the ♠K remained in dummy as an entry to cash it. Making 6♣, plus 1370.

"I should have sacrificed in six hearts," mumbled West.

Not so. Even on favorable vulnerability, minus 800 would save only 2 IMPs when 6♣ made, but could turn a wash into a 14-IMP loss if 6♣ failed. Bucking 14-to-2 odds is just bad bridge.

DEAL 41. USING YOUR ENTRIES
WHEN YOU NEED THEM

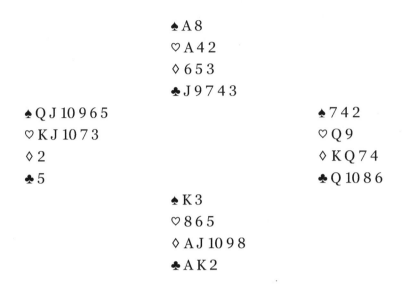

```
                    ♠ A 8
                    ♡ A 4 2
                    ◊ 6 5 3
                    ♣ J 9 7 4 3
♠ Q J 10 9 6 5                        ♠ 7 4 2
♡ K J 10 7 3                          ♡ Q 9
◊ 2                                   ◊ K Q 7 4
♣ 5                                   ♣ Q 10 8 6
                    ♠ K 3
                    ♡ 8 6 5
                    ◊ A J 10 9 8
                    ♣ A K 2
```

Friends of Fred don't play Landy, Woolsey, Cappelletti or [Your Name Here] versus 1NT. They all play *Hamilton*, in which West's 2◊ over South's 1NT showed both majors. That didn't stop North from gambling 3NT.

West led the ♠Q. Declarer counted six top tricks, so he needed three more from one of the minors. Dropping a doubleton ♣Q was very much against the odds, but he could bring the diamonds home unless West had both missing honors. That too was very much against the odds.

Therefore, declarer won the opening lead in dummy to lead low to his ◊J, which won as both defenders followed low. Cross to dummy's ♡A to repeat the finesse? Not a good idea to release the last stopper!

So declarer laid the ◊A down. Oops, West showed out. When the smoke cleared, declarer had only seven tricks. Down two.

How would you have timed the play?

The declarer in the other room knew how. After the same start, upon winning the ◊J, he led the ◊10, surrendering a diamond trick early. Now dummy's ♡A remained as an entry to repeat the diamond finesse after East returned a spade to declarer's ♠K.

Surrender a trick you must lose early, repeat a marked finesse later.

DEAL 42. SUIT ESTABLISHMENT
WITH ENTRY PROBLEMS

<pre>
                        ♠ A 8 2
                        ♡ K Q J 8 4
                        ◇ 10 8 5 2
                        ♣ A
       ♠ 9 7   ♠ Q J 10 4
       ♡ 9 7   ♡ A 10 6 5
       ◇ Q J 7 6   ◇ K
       ♣ J 10 9 4 3   ♣ 8 6 5 2
                        ♠ K 6 5 3
                        ♡ 3 2
                        ◇ A 9 4 3
                        ♣ K Q 7
</pre>

After 1◇-1♡,1♠-2♣ (artificial and forcing) South rebid 2NT and North put him in 3NT.

West led the ♣J to dummy's ♣A. Seeing six top tricks elsewhere, South saw that he needed three tricks from dummy's hearts. Unwilling to burn his diamond and spade entries to reach his hand to lead hearts up twice, declarer started hearts with dummy's ♡K.

Counting declarer for two hearts from the auction, East ducked. He captured dummy's ♡Q next with his ♡A and returned a club to South's ♣K.

With only one dummy entry left and hearts splitting 4-2, declarer could not both establish and cash dummy's fifth heart for a ninth trick. Down one.

Was there a way for declarer to develop *and cash* three heart tricks?

Yes, so long as he did not want *four*. In the other room, South led dummy's ♡8 to Trick 2. East took care to play the ♡10 and his club return dislodged another club stopper.

Then South led his remaining heart to dummy's ♡K and East's ♡A. Dummy's ♠A remained as the entry to three heart tricks, enough for nine tricks in all.

DEAL 43. WHICH SUIT? ENTRY PROBLEMS

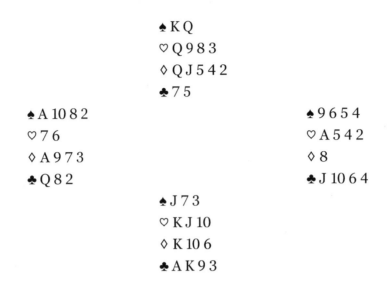

```
                      ♠ K Q
                      ♡ Q 9 8 3
                      ◊ Q J 5 4 2
                      ♣ 7 5
     ♠ A 10 8 2                        ♠ 9 6 5 4
     ♡ 7 6                             ♡ A 5 4 2
     ◊ A 9 7 3                         ◊ 8
     ♣ Q 8 2                           ♣ J 10 6 4
                      ♠ J 7 3
                      ♡ K J 10
                      ◊ K 10 6
                      ♣ A K 9 3
```

Despite North's use of Stayman, West led a fourth-highest ♠2 against South's normal but threadbare 3NT. Seeing four diamond tricks to be developed but only three tricks possible in hearts, declarer attacked the more promising diamond suit. West let him hold the ◊K and ◊10, and won the third diamond.

When West continued with the ♠A and then the ♠8, South won the ♠J. He tried the ♡K followed by the ♡J, but East ducked twice, saving his ♡A to capture dummy's ♡Q, declarer's last hope for a dummy entry.

Down one, with only two tricks in each suit.

Did declarer do anything wrong?

This declarer did, but not the South in the other room. Needing only three tricks from a red suit, he left the suit with the sure entry untouched. Instead he drove out the ace of the entryless suit, hearts. East waited until the third heart to take his ♡A.

When South won the third spade with his ♠J, he led the ◊K. West ducked, but now a low diamond forced a diamond entry to dummy.

The defenders took only three aces and a long spade. 3NT made.

DEAL 44. LIMITED DUMMY ENTRY PROBLEMS

```
                      ♠ 5 4 2
                      ♡ J 4 2
                      ◊ A K 8 7 5
                      ♣ 10 7
    ♠ Q J 10 7 6                        ♠ 9 3
    ♡ 3                                 ♡ 10 8 5
    ◊ 10 4                              ◊ Q J 9 3
    ♣ K 8 6 5 2                         ♣ Q 9 4 3
                      ♠ A K 8
                      ♡ A K Q 9 7 6
                      ◊ 6 2
                      ♣ A J
```

After a strong artificial 2♣ opening and 2♡ rebid, South landed in 6♡. He won West's obvious ♠Q lead with the ♠A. Hoping for a 3-3 diamond split, he cashed dummy's top diamonds and ruffed a third diamond high.

Alas, in the absence of a second dummy entry, the 4-2 diamond split meant down one.

Could you handle the 4-2 diamond split to make this slam?

In the other room, South reached the same slam but did not want to rely on 3-3 diamonds, only a 36% chance. He won the ace of spades and ace of hearts, as both defenders followed. Then he tried an 84% play, ducking a diamond all around.

East's club shift did declarer no harm. South won the ♣A and ♡K. Then he crossed to dummy's ◊K and ruffed a low diamond with his ♡Q.
A trump to dummy's ♡J drew East's last trump and left him in dummy.

Dummy's ◊A8 provided discards for declarer's ♠8 and ♣J. South made 6♡.

DEAL 45. ENTRIES ARE FOR ENTERING

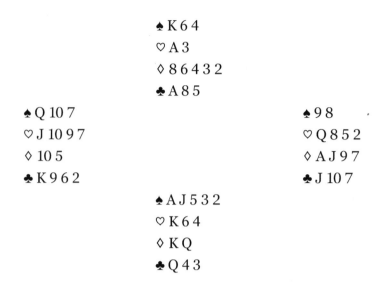

```
                      ♠ K 6 4
                      ♡ A 3
                      ◊ 8 6 4 3 2
                      ♣ A 8 5
      ♠ Q 10 7                        ♠ 9 8
      ♡ J 10 9 7                      ♡ Q 8 5 2
      ◊ 10 5                          ◊ A J 9 7
      ♣ K 9 6 2                       ♣ J 10 7
                      ♠ A J 5 3 2
                      ♡ K 6 4
                      ◊ K Q
                      ♣ Q 4 3
```

South refrained wisely from straining to open 1NT. He opened 1♠ and reached 4♠ via a "forcing notrump" auction.

West led the ♡J and South relied on at least one of two suits to work, hoping for either ♠Q or the ♣K to be with East and for spades to split 3-2.

Declarer took the ♡A and ♡K, then ruffed a heart in dummy. As West held a guarded ♠Q and the ♣K, declarer lost a spade and two clubs on finesses, along with the ◊A. Down one.

Jim wrote a whole book on finesses, advising: *try to avoid them*. Could you?

South in the other room did just that. Seeing dummy's five diamonds, he won Trick 1 with his ♡K to work on setting them up. He led the ◊K; East won the ◊A and led the ♣J through.

Not imagining East to have underled the ♣K, South let the ♣J ride to dummy's ♣A. He unblocked the ◊Q, cashed the ♠A, led to dummy's ♠K, and ruffed a diamond. West could overruff or not, but dummy remained with two entries. South used the ♡A to set up the fifth diamond, and a heart ruff to lead it and shed a club loser.

"I'm glad I read Dr J's book *The Finesse, Only a Last Resort*," said South.

DEAL 46. SAVE THOSE DUMMY ENTRIES

```
                    ♠ K Q 6 4 3
                    ♡ 8 4
                    ◊ J 10 8 6
                    ♣ A 3
      ♠ 9 7                          ♠ A J 10 5
      ♡ K Q 6 3                      ♡ 10 9 7 5 2
      ◊ 7 2                          ◊ 3
      ♣ K Q 10 8 7                   ♣ J 6 5
                    ♠ 8 2
                    ♡ A J
                    ◊ A K Q 9 5 4
                    ♣ 9 4 2
```

Avoiding the notrump trap, South landed in 5◊ and received a ♣K opening lead. He won the ♣A and entered his hand with the ◊A to start spades. West gave count with the ♠9, so East knew to duck dummy's ♠Q.

Declarer returned to his hand with the ◊K, drawing the last missing trump. When he led another spade, East took dummy's ♠Q with the ♠A.

The ♣J and another club tapped dummy. Declarer ruffed a spade, but East remained with the high ♠J. South needed two dummy entries: one to ruff another spade, another to cash dummy's fifth spade.

Having only one, he lost a heart and went down one.

Overbid or mistimed? Could you have found another entry?

In the other room, declarer stayed one step ahead. At Trick 2 he led the ♠K. This saved one round of diamonds, thus creating an extra entry.

East ducked the ♠K, but then declarer led a low spade. East won cheaply and as East at the other table, continued clubs to tap dummy.

Having three trumps left in dummy, however, declarer used two to ruff spades high, and still had a third to enter dummy and dump his ♡J on the fifth spade.

Making five diamonds.

DEAL 47. "DON'T MAKE SEVEN, PARD!"

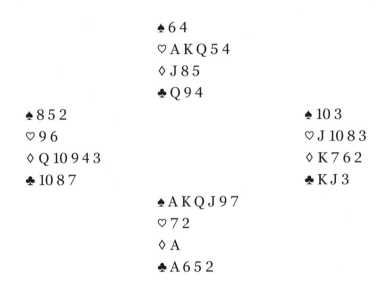

North and South were using "1430" replies to the Roman Keycard Blackwood 4NT that South bid en route to the iffy 6♠ slam, but forgetfully, North replied 5◊ instead of 5♣. When West led the ◊10, North realized that he had an ace more than shown, so as he spread the dummy, he apologized and joked, "Don't make seven, pard!"

After winning the ◊A and drawing trumps, declarer tried two chances for his slam. First he played hearts from the top, hoping for a 3-3 split. No luck there, so he ruffed the fourth heart and tried to reach dummy by leading to the ♣Q. No luck there either, so South lost two clubs. Down one.

"Can't you count to 12?" asked North as he scored it minus 100.

"If God intended us to count to 12, He'd have given us six fingers on each hand," countered South.

"If He'd wanted us to count to 13, He'd have given us six-and-a-half," sneered North.

How should a bridge player with only five fingers per hand declare?

In the other room, South reached 6♠ without benefit of Blackwood but remembered that in six he needed only 12 tricks, not 13. A 4-2 *or* 3-3 split, an 84% chance, would suffice. So he won the ◊A at Trick 1, drew trump and ducked a heart next to make 6♠ on the actual 4-2 split. Plus 1430.

"Well declared," said North. "If hearts had split three-three and you'd missed an overtrick, you'd never hear me complain."

DEAL 48. CAREFUL DUMMY ENTRY PRESERVATION

```
                    ♠ Q 7 6 5 3 2
                    ♡ Q 5
                    ◊ K J 10
                    ♣ A 8
    ♠ K 10 4                         ♠ 9 8
    ♡ 3 2                            ♡ K 4
    ◊ 8 5 2                          ◊ A 9 6 4 3
    ♣ Q J 10 7 5                     ♣ 6 4 3 2
                    ♠ A J
                    ♡ A J 10 9 8 7 6
                    ◊ Q 7
                    ♣ K 9
```

"Overstate the high-card strength or understate the playing strength?"

South guessed to overstate and soon found himself in a precarious 6♡. He captured West's ♣Q opening lead with dummy's ♣A and drew trump in two rounds with a successful finesse.

South claimed: "Knocking out the ace of diamonds and pitching a spade on dummy's third diamond."

West rejected the claim and summoned the director.

Why did the director rule down one? How should South have played?

When South claimed, he had not yet dislodged the ◊A, and he had no dummy entry left to cash dummy's third diamond after dislodging it. East could win the *second* diamond and exit in clubs, sticking declarer in his hand with no entry to the good diamond.

In the other room in the same iffy 6♡, South won Trick 1 in hand with the ♣K and overtook his ◊Q with dummy's ◊K at once. Even if East ducked, South could finesse trumps successfully and drive out the ◊A while dummy still had the ♣A as an entry.

South's play to Trick 1 was his first error. What was his second?

Claiming. Had South played on, East might not have judged to duck the first diamond, and 6♡ might have rolled home. Once declarer claimed, West was entitled to chime in, and only the defenders were presumed to play perfectly thereafter. So we advise: *Don't claim!*

DEAL 49. DON'T KILL YOUR ONLY DUMMY ENTRY

```
                      ♠ K 9 3
                      ♡ 4 2
                      ◊ K Q J 10 7 6
                      ♣ 8 5
    ♠ Q 10 7 6 4                            ♠ 8 5 2
    ♡ A 6 3                                 ♡ K 10 9
    ◊ 9                                     ◊ A 8 3
    ♣ J 10 7 3        Suki                  ♣ Q 9 6 2
                      ♠ A J
                      ♡ Q J 8 7 5
                      ◊ 5 4 2
                      ♣ A K 4
```

Lack of a happy rebid over a 1♠ response led Suki (South) to eschew a 1♡ opening in favor of a 15-17 HCP 1NT opening. North raised to 3NT.

Christmas came early for declarer as West's routine ♠6 opening lead came round to her ♠J. She grinned, turned to West and gloated, "Other teachers warn their students against leading from kings, but they're male chauvinist pigs. I tell mine never to lead from queens. Would you like to take my Monday morning classes?"

West kept silent and discarded low spades while declarer ran dummy's diamonds. Did we say "ran"? Sorry, East ducked twice and won the third diamond, then shifted to clubs.

The nine tricks with which South started shrank to seven, as dummy's last three diamonds were stranded. She lost one diamond, two clubs and three hearts. The noise South heard was North's teeth grinding.

How should South have declared?

With more thought at Trick 1. In the other room, South kept her handsome, winsome Jack, for she realized he provided the only outside entry to dummy's diamonds. No free gifts, thank you. After winning the *ace* of spades at Trick 1, she had an easy nine tricks.

You might think no one would mess up this hand, but Jim was North and it was his teeth that Suki, the feminist bridge teacher, heard gnashing.

DEAL 50. TRADE A TRICK FOR A SCARCE ENTRY

$\spadesuit$ A 7 2
$\heartsuit$ J 10 9
$\diamond$ J 9 4 3 2
$\clubsuit$ 4 2

$\spadesuit$ Q 9 8 3 $\spadesuit$ J 6 5 4
$\heartsuit$ Q 6 5 4 3 $\heartsuit$ A 2
$\diamond$ A 10 $\diamond$ K 8 7 5
$\clubsuit$ 9 7 $\clubsuit$ K 8 5

$\spadesuit$ K 10
$\heartsuit$ K 8 7
$\diamond$ Q 6
$\clubsuit$ A Q J 10 6 3

We do not endorse opening 1NT with a six-card minor as a general practice, but South ran into trouble after opening 1$\clubsuit$ here. After North responded 1$\diamond$, she thought her hand too strong for 2$\clubsuit$ and couldn't resist jumping to 2NT. North raised to 3NT. Perhaps hands like South's call for a 1NT opening as the least of evils after all.

East won West's $\heartsuit$4 opening lead with the $\heartsuit$A and returned the $\heartsuit$2 to South's $\heartsuit$K. Declarer crossed to dummy's $\spadesuit$A to finesse the $\clubsuit$Q. The finesse won but declarer had no reentry to dummy to repeat it.

When the $\clubsuit$K did not fall beneath South $\clubsuit$A next, there was blood on the table: hers. She could no longer make 1NT, let alone 3NT.

How did the declarer in the other room make two overtricks after her 1NT opening bought the contract?

By dropping the $\heartsuit$K under East's $\heartsuit$A at Trick 1. Trading one trick to gain three or four? Not really. She still scored a heart trick, but in dummy, where she wanted to be, and two club finesses led to nine tricks.

DEAL 51. HOW MANY IS ENOUGH?

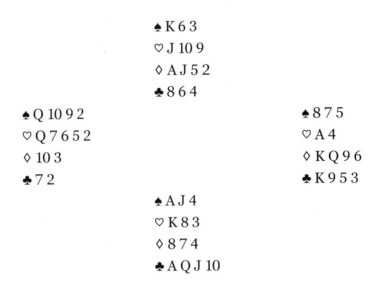

```
                        ♠ K 6 3
                        ♡ J 10 9
                        ◊ A J 5 2
                        ♣ 8 6 4
   ♠ Q 10 9 2                              ♠ 8 7 5
   ♡ Q 7 6 5 2                             ♡ A 4
   ◊ 10 3                                  ◊ K Q 9 6
   ♣ 7 2                                   ♣ K 9 5 3
                        ♠ A J 4
                        ♡ K 8 3
                        ◊ 8 7 4
                        ♣ A Q J 10
```

Allowing for South's possible minimum 1NT opening, North invited game with a simple 2NT raise. Of course South passed.

West led the ♡5 to East's ♡A. Having flubbed a previous 3NT, South counted her dummy entries, noticed the ◊A and ♠K, and said, "No problem this time, as I have *two* dummy entries *outside* of hearts."

"So you don't want to unblock hearts? Very well then, I'll let you score your precious king or queen," said East as he returned the ♡4.

South crossed to dummy's ♠K and finessed clubs successfully. She returned to dummy's ◊A and repeated the club finesse. However, when West discarded a club on the ♣A, South found herself an entry short and a trick short. Whoops, no 2NT.

What can we learn from this?

Neither of us can remember whether it was Homer Simpson or Wallis Simpson who said, "You can never be too rich or too thin," but both of us say, *you can never have too many entries.*

Declaring the same contract in the other room, South appreciated this. Just in case he needed to finesse clubs three times, he threw his ♡K under East's ♡A at Trick 1. Eventually, he scored the eight tricks he needed to make 2NT.

DEAL 52. PRESERVING DUMMY'S ENTRIES BY UNBLOCKING

```
                  ♠ A Q 10
                  ♡ Q 8 6
                  ◊ 7 6 5 4
                  ♣ 5 4 2
♠ 9 7 4 3 2                        ♠ 6 5
♡ 5                               ♡ K 4 3 2
◊ K Q J 3 2                        ◊ 10 9 8
♣ 10 8                            ♣ K 9 7 6
                  ♠ K J 9
                  ♡ A J 10 9 7
                  ◊ A
                  ♣ A Q J 3
```

North had pulled the 3♡ card from her bidding box when she meant to raise South's 1♡ opening to 2♡. When she noticed, it was too late to correct, as South had already bid 6♡.

The absence of wasted diamond face cards left declarer with some slim hope in 6♡. He won the diamond lead and led low to dummy's ♠10. Then he let dummy's ♡Q ride for a successful finesse.

After leading low to his ♡J and seeing West show out, he overtook his ♠J with dummy's ♠Q to take a third heart finesse and then draw East's last trump.

Time for clubs. Spraining his left shoulder to pat himself on the back for his careful preservation of spade entries, he crossed to dummy to start clubs. The ♣Q won, but as East's ♣K was thrice guarded, declarer lost two club tricks at the end.

Was there any way for declarer to hold his club losers to one?

In the other room, North-South stopped in 4♡ on a normal auction. South exercised good technique, even with only an overtrick IMP at stake. After crossing to dummy's ♠10 at Trick 2, he let the ♡8 ride. Then he continued with the ♡Q, remaining in dummy for a third heart finesse.

He cashed the ♡A and crossed to dummy twice more in spades to finesse clubs twice and take 12 tricks.

DEAL 53. LIMITED ENTRIES AND SPOT CARDS

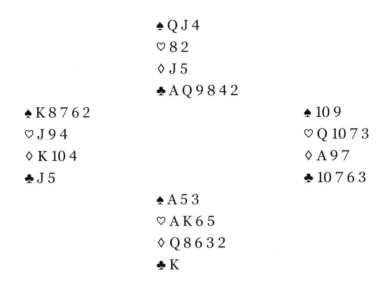

♠ Q J 4
♥ 8 2
♦ J 5
♣ A Q 9 8 4 2

♠ K 8 7 6 2
♥ J 9 4
♦ K 10 4
♣ J 5

♠ 10 9
♥ Q 10 7 3
♦ A 9 7
♣ 10 7 6 3

♠ A 5 3
♥ A K 6 5
♦ Q 8 6 3 2
♣ K

Perhaps wary of rebid problems after opening 1♦ and ordered by a rigid partner never to open 1♥ with only four, or perhaps from sheer notrump hoggery, South opened 1NT. North raised to 3NT.

Declarer did well to let West's ♠6 opening lead ride to his ♠A, saving dummy's ♠QJ for an entry to the clubs. Then he unblocked the ♣K and led low to dummy's ♣J, which won as West graciously ducked.

When clubs split 4-2, dummy's three remaining clubs died on the vine, and declarer fell two tricks short.

Could you have found some hidden assets to bring 3NT home?

The South in the other room, a confirmed Notrump Sow, reached 3NT by the same route. Counting two tricks in each major, she needed only five tricks from clubs and could afford to lose a club even if the suit split 3-3. She too took care to win Trick 1 with the ♠A.

If clubs split 4-2 with at least one honor in the short hand, nearly a 30% extra chance, dummy's lovely spot-cards, the ♣9 and ♣8, could drive out a missing honor and see her home.

Accordingly, she overtook her ♣K with dummy's ♣A to be able to continue clubs, and was rewarded when the ♣J fell graciously under dummy's ♣Q. Dummy's ♣9 dislodged East's ♣10, and nine tricks rolled in.

DEAL 54. ONE GOOD PLAY MAY NOT SUFFICE

```
                        ♠ Q J 4
                        ♡ 9 7 2
                        ◇ 8
                        ♣ A J 10 9 8 4
        ♠ 10 8 7 6                          ♠ K 9 3
        ♡ Q 10 6 3                          ♡ J 8
        ◇ J 5 3                             ◇ Q 10 7 6
        ♣ 6 5                               ♣ Q 7 3 2
                        ♠ A 5 2
                        ♡ A K 5 4
                        ◇ A K 9 4 2
                        ♣ K
```

Will notrump hoggery never cease? This time South had a good excuse for opening 2NT: a reasonable fear of being marooned in one of whichever red suit he might otherwise open. North might have sought a club slam but settled for a 3NT raise.

West must have been a disciple of Suki, the bridge teacher who told her students, "Never lead from a queen," for instead of the normal ♡3 he chose a passive second-high-from-length-and-weakness ♠8.

Declarer played dummy's ♠Q to induce a cover, but East ducked. To avoid blockage, declarer then started clubs with dummy's ♣A and continued with dummy's ♣J. East took the ♣Q and shifted to the ♡J.

Declarer was locked out of dummy and finished down one.

"Bad luck," said North.

What happened to the dummy entry?

At the other table, West was Suki herself. She also led the ♠8, but South ensured an outside entry to dummy by playing low, his first good play. Then to lock up the contract, he overtook the ♣K with dummy's ♣A to continue clubs. Dummy's remaining ♠QJ provided a sure entry to the long clubs. Eleven tricks.

"Bad luck," said North. "Had the queen of clubs fallen under the ace, you'd have taken twelve tricks."

DEAL 55. "OH, LOUIS WAS THE KING OF FRANCE BEFORE ..."

```
                    ♠ 9 5 4 3 2
                    ♡ A 2
                    ◇ K 3
                    ♣ Q 10 5 4
    ♠ void                             ♠ A J 10
    ♡ 8 6 5                            ♡ Q J 10 9 7 4 3
    ◇ J 10 9 7 6                       ◇ 2
    ♣ J 9 7 6 2                        ♣ 8 3
                    ♠ K Q 8 7 6
                    ♡ K
                    ◇ A Q 8 5 4
                    ♣ A K
```

After opening 1♠ as dealer and receiving a limit raise, South reached 6♠ despite vigorous competition in hearts. He let West's heart lead ride to his ♡K, entered dummy with the ◇K, and started trumps, capturing East's ♠10 with his ♠K.

When West showed out, South was desperate to return to dummy for a second trump lead. He cashed the ◇A and—wait a minute, it didn't cash. West ruffed with the ♠J, and declarer soon conceded down one.

Careless, greedy, or just playing too quickly?

Probably all three. Yes, with all suits splitting evenly, declarer could count 14 tricks: two hearts, three clubs, four spades and five diamonds, but even splits are not guaranteed, especially after highly contested auctions.

The less greedy South who declared 6♠ in the other room was willing to settle for 12 tricks. She saw that she had more than enough winners and needed only to avoid a second trump loser. Beheading King Louis with dummy's ♡A at Trick 1, she led to her ♠K.

When West showed out, she needed only one more dummy entry to lead a second spade towards her hand. The ◇K obliged, and East's ♠A at Trick 4 was the only trick for the defense.

DEAL 56. TWO NAUGHTY BOYS

♠ Q 6
♡ J 9 7 5
◊ A K 5
♣ J 10 9 4

♠ J 10 9 8 5   ♠ K 7 3 2
♡ K 4 2   ♡ 3
◊ Q J 4   ◊ 10 8 3 2
♣ 7 5   Notrump Sow   ♣ A 8 6 2

♠ A 4
♡ A Q 10 8 6
◊ 9 7 6
♣ K Q 3

Both sensible openings lead to 4♡: 1NT via Stayman, 1♡ via a limit raise. The Notrump Sow, of course, chose 1NT.

Hoping West's ♠J lead was top of an internal sequence, she covered his ♠J opening lead with dummy's ♠Q. No such luck. She captured East's ♠K with the ♠A and crossed to dummy's ◊K to finesse trumps. No luck there either. West won the ♡K, cashed a spade and led the ◊Q to dummy's ◊A.

.

It was too late to say you're sorry. West's ◊J became the setting trick, and East led to it upon winning the ♣A.

North hadn't been paying much attention and asked, "Another of your 14-point notrumps?"

"No, just two naughty boys. If they'd been well behaved, I'd have made six, and you'd have asked, 'Another 19-pointer?'"

What should declarer have done?

South in the other room knew. She reached 4♡ after opening 1♡. She covered West's ♠J with dummy ♠Q, and captured one of the naughty boys with the ♠A.

However, needing only ten tricks, she kept both top diamonds. She played trumps from the top promptly, and set up clubs in time to pitch a diamond. She lost only to the ♣A and the two naughty boys. Making 4♡.

DEAL 57. SAVE THAT DUMMY ENTRY

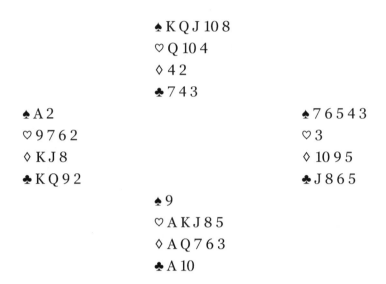

```
                    ♠ K Q J 10 8
                    ♡ Q 10 4
                    ◇ 4 2
                    ♣ 7 4 3
♠ A 2                                      ♠ 7 6 5 4 3
♡ 9 7 6 2                                  ♡ 3
◇ K J 8                                    ◇ 10 9 5
♣ K Q 9 2                                  ♣ J 8 6 5
                    ♠ 9
                    ♡ A K J 8 5
                    ◇ A Q 7 6 3
                    ♣ A 10
```

West did well to eschew the "Show the Points" double that others still use, so North-South reached 4♡ on an uncontested auction.

South captured West's ♣K opening lead with the ♣A and cashed the ♡A before leading the ♠9. West took the ♠A and ♣Q, then tapped South with a third club.

Not thinking what might go wrong, South cashed the ♡K, only to see East show out. Crossing to dummy's ♡Q, declarer tried to run spades for diamond discards. But West soon ruffed and led his last club for South to ruff with his last trump, his seventh trick. Having ◇AQ7 left, declarer could come only to one more.

Was there a way to overcome the 4-1 trump split and use dummy's spades?

In the other room, South paused to wonder: what could go wrong? Only a 4-1 trump split. So for her second trump play, she led the ♡8 to dummy's ♡10. When East showed out, she used dummy's spades to force West to ruff with his troublesome long trumps.

West did his best to exit with his fourth club, but South took care to pitch a diamond from dummy and ruff with the ♡K. She led her last trump to dummy's ♡Q and took the rest.

DEAL 58. HOW MANY WAYS TO STROKE THE CAT?

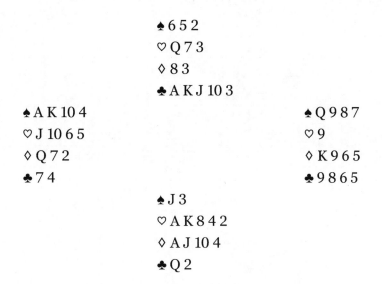

```
                    ♠ 6 5 2
                    ♡ Q 7 3
                    ◇ 8 3
                    ♣ A K J 10 3
   ♠ A K 10 4                        ♠ Q 9 8 7
   ♡ J 10 6 5                        ♡ 9
   ◇ Q 7 2                           ◇ K 9 6 5
   ♣ 7 4                             ♣ 9 8 6 5
                    ♠ J 3
                    ♡ A K 8 4 2
                    ◇ A J 10 4
                    ♣ Q 2
```

South reached 4♡ via a forcing 1NT response to 1♡ and North's 3♡ jump preference. West cashed two top spades and led a third for declarer to ruff.

"It's an easy game," thought declarer. "Draw trumps, run clubs, eleven tricks." After ruffing with the ♡2, he led low to dummy's ♡Q, winning honors first in the short hand, as he'd been taught.

He drew two more rounds with the ♡A and ♡K, and tried to run clubs, but West ruffed the third club and tapped South again with a fourth spade.

Down one. Eleven tricks had become nine.

What was a better way to handle the entries?

A kibitzer suggested cashing the ♡AK first and then running clubs, letting West ruff in while dummy still had the ♡Q as an entry. That would work, but so would the line chosen by South at the other table, where she reached 4♡ using Standard Old-Fashioned American bidding.

After she led to the ♡Q and saw East show out on the next heart, she ducked the trick to West, who was helpless to do anything more. She could ruff his spade return with dummy's remaining low trump while clubs provided entries to both hands.

Either way, an easy 10 tricks.

DEAL 59. BETTER GET A NEW
WRISTWATCH FOR BETTER TIMING

```
                    ♠ A 5 4
                    ♡ A 6 4
                    ◇ K 5 2
                    ♣ 10 9 6 2
   ♠ 9 8 3                            ♠ 7 2
   ♡ K Q 10 8                         ♡ 9 5 2
   ◇ Q 9 8 4 3                        ◇ A J 10 6
   ♣ 7                                ♣ K 8 5 4
                    ♠ K Q J 10 6
                    ♡ J 7 3
                    ◇ 7
                    ♣ A Q J 3
```

North showed a "three-card limit raise" (an oxymoron?) via a forcing 1NT response and a 3♠ jump over South's 2◇ rebid. South bid 4♠.

West led the ♡K. Declarer did well to play low from dummy. East discouraged with the ♡2, and West did well to shift to the ◇4. East won the ◇10 and returned the ♡9 to dummy's ♡A.

To have the lead in dummy after drawing trump, South took the ♠K and ♠Q first, then led to dummy's ♠A. He let dummy's ♣10 ride and it won, but when he repeated the club finesse successfully, West showed out. Unable to reach dummy to finesse clubs a third time, South lost a club to East and went down one.

Was there a way for declarer to untangle his clubs and make?

There was, as South in the other room demonstrated. Upon winning dummy's ♡A, he finessed the ♣Q immediately. Only then did he draw trumps ending in dummy.

Finally, he let dummy's ♣10 ride and when West showed out, the lead was still in dummy. A third club finesse brought the contract home.

"Perfectly timed!" exclaimed North.

CREATING AND SAVING DECLARER'S ENTRIES

DEAL 60. WHAT PRICE FORESIGHT?

```
                        ♠ A Q 5 2
                        ♡ A J 4
                        ◇ 5 4
                        ♣ J 10 9 8
    ♠ K 4                                    ♠ J 9 8 7 6
    ♡ 10 8 7 5                               ♡ Q 9 3
    ◇ A Q J 9 7 3                            ◇ 10 8 2
    ♣ 3                                      ♣ Q 5
                        ♠ 10 3
                        ♡ K 6 2
                        ◇ K 6
                        ♣ A K 7 6 4 2
```

West's vulnerable 1◇ overcall didn't keep his opponents from driving to 3NT, but his passive ♡8 opening lead didn't help declarer make it.

South suspected that West had led from the ♡Q. A second-round heart finesse could be fatal if it lost, so declarer tried dummy's ♡J at Trick 1. East covered with the ♡Q and South won the ♡K.

The ♣Q didn't fall under the ♣A on the first round, but South took comfort in the knowledge that she would fall under the ♣K next. She did, but the clubs were blocked. South could win only four clubs, not six. He soldiered on with a spade finesse and two more clubs.

Down to ♡107 and ◇AQJ9, West followed low to the ♡A next. Soon West found himself on lead with the ♡10. He could do no more than cash the ◇A before putting declarer in with the ◇K. Eight tricks became 11.

Who went wrong?

Both South and West erred.

South erred at Trick 1, failing to play dummy's ♡A to save his ♡K as an entry and keeping East, the danger hand, off lead. West erred by neglecting to unload his ♡10, a card with which he could be thrown in; he needed to rely on East to have the ♡9 for an *entry*.

In the other room, South took dummy's ♡A at Trick 1 and romped home with nine tricks: one spade, two hearts, and six clubs. No justice!

DEAL 61. COMBINE YOUR CHANCES
BUT WATCH YOUR ENTRIES

```
                        ♠ 4 3
                        ♡ A 4
                        ◊ A Q 10
                        ♣ A Q 10 8 5 4
    ♠ K Q 10 9 7 5                        ♠ 8 6 2
    ♡ K 10 8 5                            ♡ Q 9
    ◊ J 3                                 ◊ 9 8 5 4
    ♣ 6                                   ♣ J 9 7 3
                        ♠ A J
                        ♡ J 7 6 3 2
                        ◊ K 7 6 2
                        ♣ K 2
```

After North opened 1♣ as dealer and rebid 3♣, South bid 3NT despite the warning bell of West's spade overcall. He ducked West's ♠Q opening lead and won West's ♠9 continuation perforce. He wondered if he'd missed a slam, as he could count 12 tricks if both minors broke favorably.

Going after the longest suit first, declarer cashed the ♣K at Trick 3 and continued with the ♣2. When West discarded, it was time for Plan B, *diamonds*. If they split 3-3, nine tricks were still available.

So: ◊A, ◊Q and a short-lived sigh of relief when the ◊J fell under it. Oops, Plan B failed also, as declarer could not overtake dummy's ◊10 with his ◊K without promoting East's ◊9 to a stopper. Down one.

Could declarer have combined his chances more effectively?

In the other room, South appreciated the extra chance of the ◊J falling doubleton in either defender's hand. He noticed that the diamonds could block but the clubs could not.

So he tried his chances in the order that catered to that blockage. Testing diamonds before clubs, he was able to cash dummy's three diamond honors while he still had the ♣K as an entry to his hand.

Anticipating entry problems does the trick, on this deal the *ninth* trick.

DEAL 62. PRELIMINARY PLANNING
WITH LIMITED ENTRIES

```
                    ♠ J 9
                    ♡ K Q 9
                    ◊ K Q 10 8 2
                    ♣ J 6 2
    ♠ 10 7 5 2                        ♠ K 8 6 4 3
    ♡ A J 6                           ♡ 10 5 3 2
    ◊ J 9 6 3                         ◊ 5
    ♣ A 9                             ♣ K 10 5
                    ♠ A Q
                    ♡ 8 7 4
                    ◊ A 7 4
                    ♣ Q 8 7 4 3
```

South had nothing extra for her third-seat 1♣ opening, but wound up in game when North raised her 1NT rebid to 3NT.

After West's ♠2 opening lead scooped up East's ♠K, South saw that she needed five tricks from diamonds and two from hearts quickly. Short of entries to her hand, she started hearts immediately, leading low to dummy's ♡Q. Relieved to see it win, she returned to her hand with the ◊A to lead another heart.

This time West hopped up with the ♡A to continue spades. Dummy's ♠J fell beneath declarer's ♠Q, her last hand entry, whereupon she led to dummy's ◊Q and ... oops, East showed out. From there, South could take only one more trick, dummy's ◊K, her seventh trick. Down two.

Could declarer have foreseen the danger and planned ahead to avoid it?

Yes. In the other room, North raised only to 2NT and declarer needed only eight tricks. South cashed dummy's ◊K before returning to his ◊A, a discovery play that revealed the need to finesse in diamonds later. He wound up with nine tricks and chided himself for passing 2NT.

"No," said North. "We were high enough. Swap the East-West hands and even two notrump goes down."

DEAL 63. PRESERVING THE ENTRY TO YOUR HAND

```
                    ♠ A Q 4
                    ♡ A K
                    ◊ 8 6 5 3
                    ♣ A J 10 9
     ♠ J 9 7 6 2                      ♠ 10 8
     ♡ 8 6                            ♡ 10 9 7 5 3 2
     ◊ A K J                          ◊ 7 2
     ♣ 8 4 2                          ♣ K 7 6
                    ♠ K 5 3
                    ♡ Q J 4
                    ◊ Q 10 9 4
                    ♣ Q 5 3
```

South's standard 8-10 HCP response to 1♣ put him at the helm when North raised to 3NT. He counted three top tricks in each major, and three or four club tricks depending on the fate of the club finesse.

To be able to take that finesse, declarer won West's opening spade lead in hand. Oops, when the ♣Q lost to East's ♣K at Trick 2, nine sure tricks became eight.

Too late, as South had already burned the ♠K, his only entry to the third heart. Bad luck in the diamond suit doomed 3NT

"What happened to your nine top tricks?" asked North.

How did South safeguard her nine top tricks in the other room?

By not risking all for a 1-IMP overtrick. She won the ♠Q in dummy at Trick 1 and played clubs from the top.

No problems from there except to avoid revoking.

DEAL 64. CREATING ENTRIES TO YOUR HAND

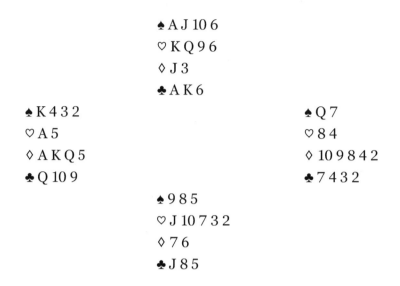

♠ A J 10 6
♥ K Q 9 6
♦ J 3
♣ A K 6

♠ K 4 3 2
♥ A 5
♦ A K Q 5
♣ Q 10 9

♠ Q 7
♥ 8 4
♦ 10 9 8 4 2
♣ 7 4 3 2

♠ 9 8 5
♥ J 10 7 3 2
♦ 7 6
♣ J 8 5

After West opened 1♦ as dealer and North doubled, competitive bidding drove South to 3♥.

West led the ♦K, promising the ♦Q, and continued with the ♦A. He cashed the ♥A and got off lead safely with his other heart. Declarer played low from dummy on both heart leads to win the second heart in hand.

When declarer started spades by floating the ♠9, East won the ♠Q and switched to clubs. South had no way back to his hand for a second spade finesse. He could do no better than play the ♠A and another to establish a fourth spade for a club discard and hold the set to down one.

Could you have found another entry to repeat the spade finesse?

The declarer in the Closed Room faced the same entry shortage as in the Open Room. But to create an extra hand entry, he dropped dummy's ♥K under West's ♥A. After winning the second heart in hand, he led the ♠5 to dummy's ♠10.

East won the ♠Q and led clubs as in the Open Room. But South overtook dummy's ♥9 with his ♥10 to lead the ♠9 and underplay dummy's Carefully Preserved ♠6.

With the lead still in hand, he repeated the spade finesse to be able to discard his club loser on dummy's fourth spade. Three hearts, bid, made and chalked up, thank you!

DEAL 65. GETTING THE BAD NEWS FIRST

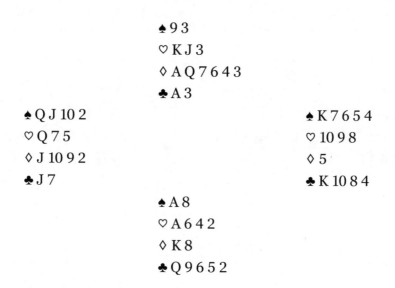

```
                    ♠ 9 3
                    ♡ K J 3
                    ◊ A Q 7 6 4 3
                    ♣ A 3
    ♠ Q J 10 2                        ♠ K 7 6 5 4
    ♡ Q 7 5                           ♡ 10 9 8
    ◊ J 10 9 2                        ◊ 5
    ♣ J 7                             ♣ K 10 8 4
                    ♠ A 8
                    ♡ A 6 4 2
                    ◊ K 8
                    ♣ Q 9 6 5 2
```

South eschewed the often awkward 2♣ response to 1◊. He bid 1♡ and did well to bid 3NT over North's 2♡ raise to offer a choice of games. Of course, having raised on three, North passed gladly. Well bid, gentlemen!

Counting nine easy tricks, South ducked West's ♠Q opening lead just to keep in practice but was forced to capture West's ♠10 continuation with the ♠A. Then, playing "short honors first," he cashed the ◊K and continued with the ◊8.

Oops, bad news first: East discarded a club. Good news next: when declarer reentered his hand with the ♡A to lead a heart up, dummy's ♡J held and West's ♡Q fell beneath dummy's ♡K. Bad news again: South had no way back to his hand to cash his long heart. Down one.

"Nine tricks off the top if you win them in the right order," said North.
"I'm getting tired of hearing that from you," replied a tired South.

What *was* the right order?

To keep his options open and entries intact, South in the other room did something odd. He blocked diamonds, taking the ◊A first and then the ◊K. Had diamonds split 3-2, he could reach dummy in hearts to run the suit.

When they split 4-1, he was in hand to finesse West for ♡Qxx, and 3NT rolled home with four hearts, three diamonds and two black aces.

DEAL 66. GIVE UP YOUR STOPPER OR YOUR ENTRY?

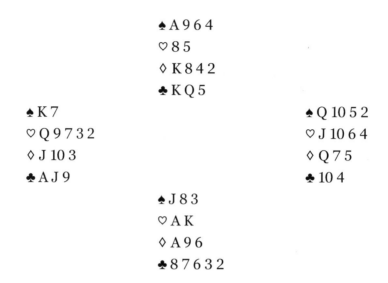

                ♠ A 9 6 4
                ♡ 8 5
                ◊ K 8 4 2
                ♣ K Q 5

♠ K 7   ♠ Q 10 5 2
♡ Q 9 7 3 2   ♡ J 10 6 4
◊ J 10 3   ◊ Q 7 5
♣ A J 9   ♣ 10 4

                ♠ J 8 3
                ♡ A K
                ◊ A 9 6
                ♣ 8 7 6 3 2

After opening 1♣ as dealer on favorable vulnerability. South couldn't stop below game and reached a very iffy 3NT. West led the ♡3.

At Trick 2. declarer started clubs by leading the ♣3 to dummy's ♣Q.

Not wanting to relinquish his lone remaining stopper in the defenders' long heart suit, he reentered his hand with the ◊A to continue clubs. Now West rose with the ♣A to continue with the ♡2, killing South's last entry to his clubs. South was lucky to go down only one.

Should declarer have used his second heart stopper early instead of burning his entry in the safe suit, diamonds?

Yes. After winning Trick 2 with dummy's ♣Q, the declarer in the other room realized that he could lose three hearts and a club and still take nine tricks. Accordingly, he abandoned the heart entry that the defenders could always remove in order to keep his invulnerable diamond entry.

Counterintuitive, but once you think about it, clear. West took the ♣A and three hearts, but now South scored his five top tricks and four clubs to make 3NT.

DEAL 67. SAVING THE ENTRY TO YOUR HAND

```
                        ♠ A K Q
                        ♡ A J 7
                        ◇ Q 10 7 5 3
        Moshe           ♣ K 10
        ♠ 6 4                               ♠ J 10 9 8 2
        ♡ 10 9 8 5 3                        ♡ Q 6 2
        ◇ 6 4                               ◇ A K J 8
        ♣ A 7 5 3                           ♣ 8
                        ♠ 7 5 3
                        ♡ K 4
                        ◇ 9 2
                        ♣ Q J 9 6 4 2
```

The unavailability of notrump openings for tweeners like North's wrong-sided 3NT. North had to open 1◇ and raise South's 1NT response to 3NT.

South queried West's ♡10 opening lead: "Zero or two higher?"

"No, could be top of an internal sequence," said East. "Moshe is so old he learned bridge from Mr. Neanderthal himself."

"You mean Ely Culbertson," corrected West.

Hoping Moshe had led from ♡Q109(xx), and dreaming of overtricks, declarer finessed dummy's ♡J. He knew that even if East had the ♡Q, he could still win the ♡K. When East covered, however, South let the ♡Q hold "to cut the defenders' transportation."

East returned the ♡6 to South's ♡K. Leading to dummy's ♣K on the first round and overtaking dummy's ♣10 on the next, South established four more club tricks. Upon winning the ♣A, Moshe shifted to spades. Declarer scored three spades, two hearts and one club. No hand entry, down three!

How should South have declared this Bridge 101 contract?

In the other room, South won the ♡A in dummy to save the ♡K entry to his hand. When the ♣K held Trick 2, declarer overtook dummy's ♣10 at Trick 3. That 30-point overtrick of which the first declarer dreamed?

The other declarer got it when West, who was not Moshe, won the ♣A and continued hearts at Trick 4.

DEAL 68. WHEN YOU NEED AN ENTRY TO YOUR HAND

West (declarer)	East (dummy)
♠ A 8 2	♠ K Q J
♡ J	♡ K Q
◊ Q J 10 6 5 4 3	◊ A 9 8
♣ 9 2	♣ A K 7 6 4

East doubled North's 3♡ opening for takeout and raised West's 5◊ jump to 6◊. North led the ♡A against 6◊ and continued with the ♡10, leaving West with two problems:

(1) What do discard on dummy's ♡K?

(2) How to reach his hand to finesse (the percentage play) in trumps?

West at this table discarded a spade on the ♡K and overtook dummy's ♠J with the ♠A to take the trump finesse. When he led the ◊Q intending to let it ride, North played the ◊K and said, "Not your turn, but I'll accept your play anyway." Why?

It was North's turn, for he had ♠void ♡A1098652 ◊K7 ♣J1083 and had trumped the ♠A with the ◊7. He was happy to accept West's out-of-turn ◊Q because for all he knew, South had a doubleton ◊J.

Declarer captured North's ◊K with dummy's ◊A. As soon as South followed with the ◊2, West showed his hand and said, "Tricks to burn."

Down one.

In the Closed Room, West also declared 6◊ on the lead of the ♡A and another heart, but having no useful discard, he ruffed the second heart.

He finessed the ◊Q successfully and claimed the rest just as quickly as his counterpart in the Open Room. But he *made* the slam.

DEAL 69. THE MIRAGE

```
                    ♠ 10 7 6 5 2
                    ♡ 4 3
                    ♢ 8 5 2
                    ♣ 10 5 4
    ♠ Q J 9 8                        ♠ A 4 3
    ♡ Q J 7 5                        ♡ 10 9 6
    ♢ 9                              ♢ Q J 10 7 6
    ♣ K Q J 7                        ♣ A 2
                    ♠ K
                    ♡ A K 8 2
                    ♢ A K 4 3
                    ♣ 9 8 6 3
```

Unfortunately for South, he was dealer. In any other seat, East would have bid diamonds ahead of him, saving him from disaster. As it was, he opened 1♢ with nobody vul, and East passed West's takeout double for penalties while lifting his handkerchief to his mouth to prevent drooling.

West led the obligatory ♢9, and South counted his tricks: four top tricks and a heart ruff in dummy came to five. If the ♠A were on side and he could slip a spade by East, that would be six: down one, not too bad.

So, ♢A, ♡AK, heart ruff in dummy, ♠2—but East, reading the distribution well, rose ♠A and continued the ♢Q. Down two.

Any way to scramble another trick?

In the other room, South faced the same problem. Had his singleton spade been a commoner—or even a queen—instead of a king, it would have been easier. If he could wait to ruff a heart in dummy, he could ruff a spade in hand.

So, ♢A, then ♠K. East was wide awake enough to win the ♠A and continue the ♢Q. South won the ♢K, ruffed a heart with dummy's ♢8 and was in dummy just when he needed to be to ruff a spade in hand.

Down one for a neat 5-IMP pickup.

DEAL 70. DELAY DRAWING TRUMPS
TO CREATE AN EXTRA ENTRY

```
                        ♠ Q 10 9 7 5 2
                        ♡ A 10 6
                        ◊ void
                        ♣ A J 8 2
      ♠ A J 4                              ♠ K 8 3
      ♡ 9 8 7 5 4 2                        ♡ K J 3
      ◊ K J 6 4                            ◊ Q 9 8 7 2
      ♣ void                               ♣ K 4
                        ♠ 6
                        ♡ Q
                        ◊ A 10 5 3
                        ♣ Q 10 9 7 6 5 3
```

After a highly competitive auction starting with North's second-seat 1♠ opening pushed South up to 5♣, East doubled. West's ♡9 lead depicted weakness in the suit, so declarer called for dummy's ♡A.

Then declarer cashed the ♣A. Disappointed that the ♣K didn't fall, he crossruffed: heart ruff, ◊A, diamond ruff, heart ruff, diamond ruff. Now he needed an entry to his hand to ruff his last diamond.

So he led a crafty ♠10 from dummy, but East alertly hopped ♠K to draw dummy's last trump. With no place to park his ◊10, declarer had to let West score the ◊K to go with East's two black kings. Down one doubled.

Could you have found the extra entry needed to make the contract?

In the other room, South was also doubled in 5♣, but he spotted the problem early. After winning dummy's ♡A at Trick 1, he ducked a spade at once to create an extra entry.

Then he could crossruff in peace while cashing dummy's ♣A along the way. He lost only one spade and one club.

DEAL 71. CREATING AN ENTRY TO YOUR HAND

```
              ♠ 8 6 4
              ♡ K Q 7
              ◇ J 9 2
              ♣ A K J 5
♠ J 10 9 5                      ♠ K 7 3 2
♡ A 5                           ♡ 10 9 8 2
◇ A Q 8 6                       ◇ 10 5 3
♣ 9 8 4                         ♣ 10 7
              ♠ A Q
              ♡ J 6 4 3
              ◇ K 7 4
              ♣ Q 6 3 2
```

After responding 1♡ to North's 1♣, South did well to rebid 2NT to invite game over North's 2♡ raise. North carried on to 3NT.

West's ♠J opening lead went to East's ♠K and South's ♠A. South started hearts by leading to dummy's ♡Q. He led low to the ♣Q to reenter his hand for another low-heart lead, but West rose with the ♡A.

West continued spades, taking care to lead the ♠9 and preserve the ♠5 as a possible fourth-round entry to East's ♠7.

Now declarer counted nine possible tricks: two spades, four clubs and three hearts. But after unblocking dummy's ♡K, he needed to catch the ◇A on side to reach his third heart trick. Sorry, West soon took the rest.

How did the declarer in the other room make 3NT?

By looking ahead to foresee the problem. After winning dummy's ♡Q at Trick 2, he cashed dummy's ♣AK. When both defenders followed, he overtook dummy's ♣J with his ♣Q.

After leading to West's ♡A next, he was able to unblock dummy's ♡K and lead to his ♣6 to cash the ♡J. He had a third heart trick to go with his six black-suit tricks.

As North lifted his palm to offer a "high five," South waved him off, saying, "No, it's a high six."

DEAL 72. PRESERVING ENTRIES TO DECLARER'S HAND

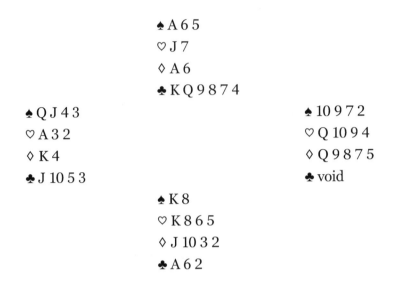

```
              ♠ A 6 5
              ♡ J 7
              ◊ A 6
              ♣ K Q 9 8 7 4
♠ Q J 4 3                          ♠ 10 9 7 2
♡ A 3 2                            ♡ Q 10 9 4
◊ K 4                             ◊ Q 9 8 7 5
♣ J 10 5 3                         ♣ void
              ♠ K 8
              ♡ K 8 6 5
              ◊ J 10 3 2
              ♣ A 6 2
```

North opened 1♣ and rebid 2♣ over South's 1♡ response. When South invited with 2 NT, North bid 3 NT. West led the ♠3.

With what looked like nine easy tricks, declarer won Trick 1 in hand with his king, as usual, playing the honor from the short side first. He cashed the ♣A and East showed out.

With every significant card unfavorably placed, nine tricks became eight. Down one. North tried hard to refrain from criticism.

How should declarer have taken his tricks?

In the other room, declaring 3NT also, South asked the time-honored question: "When everything looks too good, what can go wrong?"

Only a 4-0 club split. If East has four, tough luck. If West has four, *two* finesses will pick them up. For that, South realized, she'll need two hand entries, and she'll need use the ♣A first to find out *early.*

Accordingly, she won Trick 1 with dummy's ♠A, and led to her ♣A at Trick 2, getting the bad news.

Now she took her first club finesse, led to her carefully-preserved ♠K, and took her second finesse for nine fast tricks. Making 3NT,

TRUMPS

AS

ENTRIES

DEAL 73. MAXIMIZE YOUR TRUMP ENTRIES (1)

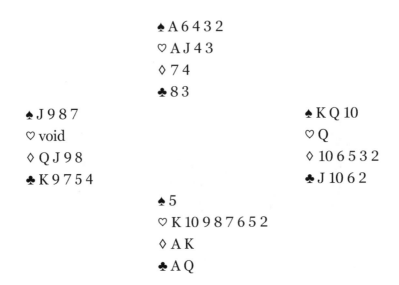

♠ A 6 4 3 2
♡ A J 4 3
◊ 7 4
♣ 8 3

♠ J 9 8 7
♡ void
◊ Q J 9 8
♣ K 9 7 5 4

♠ K Q 10
♡ Q
◊ 10 6 5 3 2
♣ J 10 6 2

♠ 5
♡ K 10 9 8 7 6 5 2
◊ A K
♣ A Q

After North's limit jump raise of his 1♡ opening, South invoked Roman Keycard Blackwood. North's 5♡ reply to 4NT showed two keys and denied the ♡Q. Hoping to catch a useful ◊Q or score his own ♣Q via a finesse or favorable opening lead, he deemed 7♡ a huge favorite and bid it forthwith.

West's ◊Q opening lead shattered South's hopes of finding that card in dummy. He drew trump with the ♡K at Trick 2 and counted his tricks. Hmmm, only 12. At this point, he saw too few dummy entries to ruff three spades and cash a long spade, so he finessed the ♣Q as his only hope.

Need we remind you of Dr J's book on finesses for you to see how that turned out? Could you have done better?

In the other room, a redhead Danny called "HH" declared 7♡. Back in the 1960s, she had played in Danny's O'Hell games and he had nicknamed her "the Hellcat Hustler."

After winning the ◊A at Trick 1, HH started spades promptly by leading to dummy's ♠A. Then she ruffed dummy's ♠6 with the ♡K, guarding against West having singletons in both majors. The ♡10 to dummy's ♡A, ♠4 ruffed high, ♡8 to dummy's ♡J, ♠3 ruffed high, and pause ...

"Danny used to say, 'Never give up the deuce,' but now I must." She led the ♡2 to dummy, threw the ♣Q on dummy's ♠2, and spread her cards.

No club hook needed.

DEAL 74. MAXIMIZE YOUR TRUMP ENTRIES (2)

```
                          ♠ 9 7 3
                          ♡ 8 6 4 3
                          ◇ Q 4 2
                          ♣ A 6 4          Uncle Walter
        ♠ 4                                ♠ A 5
        ♡ K Q J 2                          ♡ 10 9 7 5
        ◇ 10 8 6                           ◇ K J 7 5
        ♣ J 9 8 3 2                        ♣ K 10 7
                          ♠ K Q J 10 8 6 2
                          ♡ A
                          ◇ A 9 3
                          ♣ Q 5
```

We can't say we approve of Uncle Walter's "third seat" 1◇ opening. He may have bid it because he believed East would do so in the other room. Walter often thought that way. Here the shaded opening catapulted South into an iffy 4♠. Did South think it a "good save" against a feared 4♡?

Declarer won the ♡A at Trick 1 and led the ♠K to Trick 2. That was an offer Uncle Walter could and did refuse. With only a third-round ♠9 for a dummy entry, declarer could not both lead towards his ♣Q and cash dummy's ♣A to discard a diamond.

Not surprisingly, when he led to dummy's ◇Q, it lost to East's ◇K. East cashed the ♠A and exited in hearts.

Could you have wangled a second club trick to make 4♠?

In the other room, a more thoughtful declarer started trumps by leading the ♠8 to the ♠9. East had no winning option.

If East ducked, declarer would lead a club. East could win the ♣K, but declarer could cash the ♣Q and lead the ♠2 to dummy's ♠7, then discard a diamond on dummy's ♣A.

If East won the ♠A, declarer would have two trump entries to dummy with the same effect.

DEAL 75. TRUMPS ARE YOUR ONLY ENTRIES

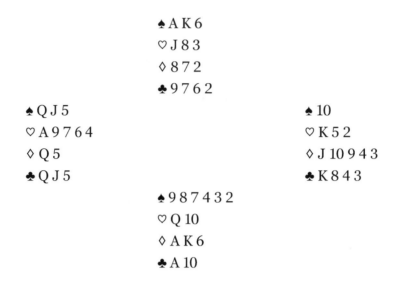

```
                    ♠ A K 6
                    ♡ J 8 3
                    ◊ 8 7 2
                    ♣ 9 7 6 2
   ♠ Q J 5                          ♠ 10
   ♡ A 9 7 6 4                      ♡ K 5 2
   ◊ Q 5                            ◊ J 10 9 4 3
   ♣ Q J 5                          ♣ K 8 4 3
                    ♠ 9 8 7 4 3 2
                    ♡ Q 10
                    ◊ A K 6
                    ♣ A 10
```

Neither side being vulnerable led both sides to push and shove in the auction. Our friend Marty Bergen, whose book on Hand Evaluation is well worth reading, would cringe at the 1♡ opening West dredged up as dealer, for he had a skinny suit and a collection of queens and jacks.

Our friend Mike Lawrence, whose book on Opening Leads is equally outstanding, might shudder with fear at South bidding 2♠ over East's 2♡ raise, lest North lead spades against a heart contract. That didn't happen, for North raised to 3♠.

Declarer counted 10 tricks if all went well. He won the opening ♣Q lead and cashed both top trumps. When East showed out on the second spade, South could set up a trick for dummy's ♡J, but he had no dummy entry to cash it. The 10 tricks he fancied shrank not to nine but to eight.

How did South in the other room find a ninth trick to make 3♠?

With good timing, of course. He attacked hearts immediately, before burning his two trump entries to dummy. The defenders could set up a trick in either minor, but not both. Declarer discarded his loser in the other minor.

Staying one step ahead, declarer won the race for the pivotal trick, to which dummy's strong trumps ensured an entry.

DEAL 76. TRUMPS AS AN ENTRY

```
                    ♠ K Q J 8
                    ♡ 8 7 3
                    ◊ J 5 2
                    ♣ K 6 5
  ♠ 7 6 4 3 2                         ♠ A 10 9
  ♡ void                              ♡ 9 6 4
  ◊ 10 9 8 7                          ◊ Q 6 4 3
  ♣ Q 9 8 2                           ♣ A 10 7
                    ♠ 5
                    ♡ A K Q J 10 5 2
                    ◊ A K
                    ♣ J 4 3
```

After two passes, South preempted with an over-strength 4♡. Not knowing of North's strong spades opposite, he had to fear a "favorable vulnerability" spade sacrifice over any slower path to 4♡.

Declarer won the opening lead with the ◊K, "advertising" the ◊A. He drew trumps and led the ♠5. West had already signaled odd count by discarding three spades up the line. When he followed with a fourth, East knew to win the ♠A immediately.

South's advertisement failed to fool his customer. East exited with the ◊3, leaving South to choose his clubs without even any advice from a caddy. Dummy's good spades rotted on the vine.

How did the crafty South in the other room score two spade tricks?

In golf, nobody asks how far you drive the ball with each swing, it's how many strokes you take that earns the par. Likewise in bridge; if you take ten tricks and make 4♡, it matters not which three tricks you lose.

In the other room, South won the ◊K and saw West show out on the ♡A. She realized she could trade one heart trick for two spade tricks. Abandoning trumps temporarily, she drove out East's ♠A with dummy's ♠J.

She won his ◊3 return and led the ♡5 to dummy's ♡7. Surprised to win the ♡9, East exited with the ◊Q, but South ruffed high and led the ♡2.

What is it Danny says about the eight of trumps? Here it was an entry to dummy's two good spades, declarer's ninth and tenth tricks. A par deal.

DEAL 77. DRAWING TRUMPS WHILE USING THEM AS ENTRIES

```
                    ♠ 7 6 4 3 2
                    ♡ Q 10 8
                    ◇ A 3
                    ♣ 7 5 2
♠ Q J 10                              ♠ K 9 8 5
♡ J 7 5                               ♡ void
◇ 10 9 7 4                            ◇ K Q 8 5 2
♣ A 9 6                               ♣ K Q 4 3
                    ♠ A
                    ♡ A K 9 6 4 3 2
                    ◇ J 6
                    ♣ J 10 8
```

East's takeout double of North's 2♡ raise did not keep South from continuing to 4♡. West's ♠Q opening lead dislodged South's ♠A.

Prospects looked grim for South, as dummy had nothing to ruff. He drew trumps and went quietly down one.

How did South make four hearts in the other room?

The Hellcat Hustler loved five-card side suits almost as much as she loved deuces, and dummy had both. East's choice to double instead of overcalling 2♠ suggested that he had four spades, so dummy's spades figured to come home. Strength is nice, but length can do in a pinch.

Unfortunately, dummy had only two trump entries when HH needed three to ruff out spades. Dummy's ◇A was an entry to cash the fifth spade.

Two glimmers of hope:

(1) Dummy had three trump entries if East's likely singleton heart were the ♡J and she led first to dummy's ♡Q.

(2) Dummy had three trump entries also if East were void and she inserted dummy's ♡8 on the first round. Each seemed about equally likely.

Which to try, the drop or the finesse? Was the extra undertrick if the finesse lost a tie-breaker?

An illusion, not a tie. For three trump entries, HH needed to finesse even if East had a low singleton. So she hooked the ♡8 on the first round and the ♡10 on the second to ruff out the spades. Oh yes, she preserved dummy's ♠2 to discard the ◇6 and take 10 tricks in the end. Making 4♡.

DEAL 78. PRESERVING AN ENTRY
TO DECLARER'S HAND

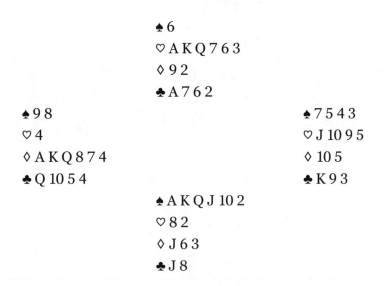

```
                    ♠ 6
                    ♡ A K Q 7 6 3
                    ◊ 9 2
                    ♣ A 7 6 2
    ♠ 9 8                              ♠ 7 5 4 3
    ♡ 4                                ♡ J 10 9 5
    ◊ A K Q 8 7 4                      ◊ 10 5
    ♣ Q 10 5 4                         ♣ K 9 3
                    ♠ A K Q J 10 2
                    ♡ 8 2
                    ◊ J 6 3
                    ♣ J 8
```

If you think this deal belongs in 4♡, the partnership's longer combined suit, instead of 4♠, think again. The best suit in which to play a misfit is the suit of the weaker hand, the hand to which trumps are needed as entries.

So South, who opened 1♠, did well to insist on 4♠ after North showed a strong hand with six hearts and four clubs over West's 2◊ overcall.

Using Patriarch Opening Leads, in which the king shows the queen, West led the ◊K and cashed the ◊A before continuing with the ◊Q. East, who had followed high-low, overruffed dummy and shifted to the ♣3. West covered South's card to drive out dummy's ♣A.

Suddenly, declarer was in trouble. He could not get to his hand to draw trumps. When he played dummy's hearts from the top to try for a club discard, West ruffed the second round and cashed a club. Declarer went down two, taking only eight tricks on a deal where he had ten.

Do you see how declarer could have taken all ten?

Barry Rigal showed a similar theme in a bridge column cited also by Mike Lawrence. The two fine analysts explained that by ruffing Trick 3 in dummy, South destroyed the one card he could use to reach his hand and draw trump. All he had to do was discard.

DEAL 79. TRUMP ENTRIES FOR THE SECOND SUIT

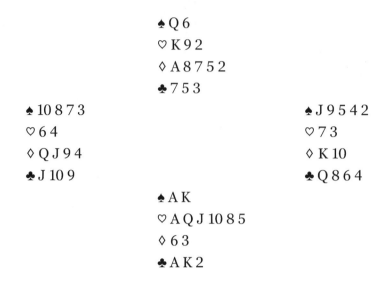

♠ Q 6
♡ K 9 2
◊ A 8 7 5 2
♣ 7 5 3

♠ 10 8 7 3
♡ 6 4
◊ Q J 9 4
♣ J 10 9

♠ J 9 5 4 2
♡ 7 3
◊ K 10
♣ Q 8 6 4

♠ A K
♡ A Q J 10 8 5
◊ 6 3
♣ A K 2

The duplicated lengths in both black suits and self-duplication of the doubleton ♠Q made this 6♡ slam not quite a slam dunk.

South captured West's ♣J opening lead with the ♣A and drew trump with the ♡A and ♡Q. Then he thought how to get rid of his club loser.

He prayed for 3-3 diamonds, ducking a diamond to East first to preserve dummy's ◊A as an entry. Upon winning East's return, he led to the ◊A and ruffed a diamond, but one ruff did not suffice to set the suit up.

After using dummy's ♡K as an entry to ruff another diamond, declarer could not find his way back to dummy to discard his ♣2 on dummy's fifth diamond. Down one.

How would you have managed your entries?

The declarer in the other room believed in the power of care, not prayer. To preserve two dummy entries in case diamonds split 4-2, he ducked a diamond promptly at Trick 2.

Upon regaining the lead, he cashed the ♡A, led to dummy's ◊A and ruffed a third diamond high. Then he crossed to dummy's ♡9 and ruffed a fourth diamond high. Dummy's ♡K remained as an entry to the long diamond on which he pitched the ♣2.

DEAL 80. WATCH YOUR TRUMP SPOTS

```
                    ♠ 10 8 4
                    ♡ Q 7 6
                    ◊ A 5 3
                    ♣ K Q 5 3
    ♠ 2                           ♠ K 7 6 5
    ♡ K J 10 4 3 2                ♡ A 9 8
    ◊ 9 8                         ◊ J 10 7 2
    ♣ 10 9 7 6                    ♣ 8 2
                    ♠ A Q J 9 3
                    ♡ 5
                    ◊ K Q 6 4
                    ♣ A J 4
```

West's "favorable vulnerability skinny mini" Weak 2♡ bid as dealer and East's "premature save" 4♡ goaded South into an iffy 6♠ after North raised his 4♠ to 5♠.

West's ♡J opening lead held Trick 1, but South ruffed the next heart low and crossed to dummy's ◊A to start trumps.

Declarer took care to lead dummy's ♠10 so he could underplay his ♠9 when East followed low. Breathing a sigh of relief when the ♠10 won, he repeated the successful trump finesse, but when West showed out he muttered "Just my luck!"

After entering dummy with the ♣Q to finish trumps with a third finesse, South realized that the clubs were blocked. When neither minor split 3-3, he conceded down one, muttering "Just my luck!" again.

Could you have avoided the fatal club blockage?

In the other room, South, pushed to the same contract, remembered a saying of Danny's: "The eight of trumps is the most underrated card in bridge." She foresaw the entry problem and ruffed with the ♠J at Trick 2.

Now she could underplay twice—first the ♠8 and then the ♠10—to remain in dummy and take a third trump finesse without burning a precious club entry. Slam, bam, thank you, Ma'am!

USING THE OPPONENTS

DEAL 81. THE BLACKWOOD JINX

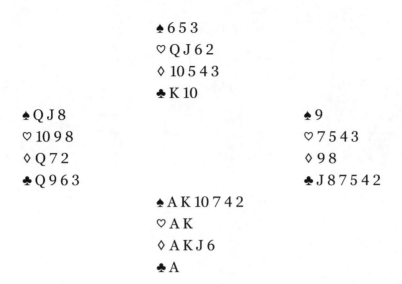

```
                    ♠ 6 5 3
                    ♡ Q J 6 2
                    ◊ 10 5 4 3
                    ♣ K 10
    ♠ Q J 8                         ♠ 9
    ♡ 10 9 8                        ♡ 7 5 4 3
    ◊ Q 7 2                         ◊ 9 8
    ♣ Q 9 6 3                       ♣ J 8 7 5 4 2
                    ♠ A K 10 7 4 2
                    ♡ A K
                    ◊ A K J 6
                    ♣ A
```

Eddie Kantar, who wrote more extensively about Roman Keycard Blackwood than anyone, said that usually "the strong hand asks the weak" for keys. Danny adds that RKB helps most when a weak hand asks a very strong one. Cue bids won't do when a weak hand has no ace to cue-bid.

That was true here. After South's Omnibus 2♣ opening and 2♠ and 3♠ rebids, North asked for keys with 4NT. He settled for 6♠ when South's 5♡ reply revealed the absence of the ♠Q.

West led the ♡10. South said, "Hmmm, might make seven."

"Beware the premature gloat!" moaned North.

At Trick 2, South cashed the ♠A as both defenders followed low.

"Don't show out!" begged South as he led the ♠K.

"Wouldn't dream of it," answered West, following with the ♠J.

"Sorry," said East as she completed a high-low in hearts.

Lacking a dummy entry, South flailed about, cashing the ◊AK. No luck there either. Soon West won the ♠Q and ◊Q. Down one.

"The Blackwood Jinx," mumbled North.

How did South in the other room overcome the Blackwood Jinx?

There South, Gypsy Rose Lee, won the first six tricks with the ♡A, ♠AK, ♣A, ♡K and ◊A, stripping the hand before throwing West in with the ♠Q. West exited with the ◊7 but South played dummy's ◊10 and claimed.

85

DEAL 82. FINESSE? WHAT FINESSE?

```
              ♠ K Q J 3 2
              ♡ 4 2
              ◊ 7 4 2
              ♣ A 10 9
♠ A 10 9 5 4                        ♠ 8 7 6
♡ 9 8 6                             ♡ 5
◊ 6                                 ◊ K Q J 10 9 8
♣ 6 5 4 2                           ♣ J 7 3
              ♠ void
              ♡ A K Q J 10 7 3
              ◊ A 5 3
              ♣ K Q 8
```

East opened a Weak 2◊ Bid on favorable vulnerability. Fearing a spade sacrifice, South bid 4♡ with his nine or ten playing tricks. North risked a 5♣ cue-bid. That was enough for South to gamble 6♡.

South won the ◊A at Trick 1 and drew trump. He saw that dummy's spades could provide discards for diamond losers, but he needed two dummy entries. One to take a ruffing finesse in spades and another to reach the two spade winners he would have regardless of the outcome of that ruffing finesse.

Having read Dr J's book on Finesses, he thought to manufacture a second dummy entry by finessing West for the ♣J. So he led the ♣8 and overtook with dummy's ♣9 when West followed low.

Oops, East won the ♣J and cashed two diamonds. Down two, -200.

"Well played," said North sympathetically. "You took a fifty percent finesse that risked only two IMPs to save 16, a chance well worth taking,"

In the other room, Moshe stumbled into 6♡ similarly and took the only finesse that could work: against West's ♠A. He won the ◊A, drew trump, overtook his ♣K with dummy's ♣A and let dummy's ♠K ride, discarding the ◊3. West won as expected, but the defense was finished. A spade or club return gave declarer access to dummy's spades.

Mightn't finessing West for the ♣J have worked too, as North and South there both supposed?

No, as West could cover South's ♣8 with the ♣J if she had it.

DEAL 83. DEUCES HAVE THEIR USES

```
                    ♠ 10 8 5
                    ♡ Q J 10 7
                    ◇ 8 6 3
                    ♣ J 10 3
    ♠ K J 6 3                      ♠ 9 7 4
    ♡ 6 4 3                        ♡ 9 8 5 2
    ◇ void                         ◇ 9 5 4
    ♣ A K Q 7 6 4                  ♣ 9 8 5
                    ♠ A Q 2
                    ♡ A K
                    ◇ A K Q J 10 7 2
                    ♣ 2
```

When West's 1♣ opening came round to him, South bid 5◇ directly. As little as the ♠J in dummy could make it a lock.

West led the ♣K and continued the ♣A. South ruffed, drew trumps, unblocked hearts and ran more diamonds. He came down to a four-card ending with the ◇7 and all three of his spades while dummy remained with ♠1086 and the ♡Q.

South exited with the ♠2, but West won the ♠J and led the ♣Q. South ruffed but had to lose Trick 13 to West's ♠K. Down one.

Could you have rescued dummy's heart winners?

Declaring 5◇ in the other room, South ruffed the second club with her ◇A. When West showed out on the ◇K next, she unblocked her hearts and led the ◇2 to dummy's ◇6.

East won the ◇9 and shifted to the ♠9, but South won the ♠A. Now he led the ◇7 to dummy's ◇8, and discarded spades on dummy's ♡QJ to take the rest.

North, who hadn't paid close attention to the play, said, "What? You lost a trump trick? Next time we cut on the same team, I'm picking another partner."

DEAL 84. THE BLACKWOOD PARADOX

```
                      ♠ A 9 7 3 2
                      ♡ 10 8
                      ◊ Q 9 6
                      ♣ J 10 2
    ♠ K Q 10 6                          ♠ J 8 5 4
    ♡ J 9 5                             ♡ Q
    ◊ 8 7 4                             ◊ J 10 5 3 2
    ♣ Q 8 7                             ♣ 9 6 3
                      ♠ void
                      ♡ A K 7 6 4 3 2
                      ◊ A K               Roger
                      ♣ A K 5 4
```

South opened an Omnibus 2♣ and rebid 2♡ over North's "waiting" 2◊ reply. North showed values by bidding 2♠. After South rebid 3♡, North had nothing better to bid than 4♡. The raise inspired South to dream of slam.

What do most bad bridge players do when they dream of slam? They think for two minutes and then bid 4NT. This pair played Roman Keycard Blackwood. North replied 5◊ to show one key. With visions of a grand slam, South bid 5NT, the Specific King Ask, thinking that the ♠K would provide a thirteenth trick. When North replied 6♡, showing no king, he passed.

West's ♠K opening lead seemed helpful. South discarded one of his club losers on dummy's ♠A, and thankful for the dummy entry that West had so kindly offered, tried a club finesse to avoid another. When that lost, the unlucky 3-1 trump split doomed the slam.

"Hmmm," mused Roger the kibitzer. "The Blackwood Paradox! If North had no aces, he might have had something more useful elsewhere and the slam would have been a better one. So, if you catch no aces, bid six, but if you catch one, stop in five. I'll have to tell Danny about this!"

How did South make 6♡ in the other room?

There South reached 6♡ on a different auction. She ruffed West's ♠K lead, cashed the ♡AK, ◊AK and ♣A, then fed West his ♡J. *Any* exit provided a *timely* entry to dummy and *two* discards on the ♠A and ◊Q.

DEAL 85. RINGO'S RULE

```
                        ♠ 6 4
                        ♡ A K 8 5 2
                        ◊ J 8 2
        Moshe           ♣ J 10 7
        ♠ 10 9 3                              ♠ void
        ♡ J 9 6 4 3                           ♡ Q 10 7
        ◊ 4                                   ◊ K Q 10 9 7 6 5
        ♣ Q 9 5 2                             ♣ 8 4 3
                        ♠ A K Q J 8 7 5 2
                        ♡ void
                        ◊ A 3
                        ♣ A K 6
```

East opened 3◊ as dealer with both sides vul at IMPs. South shrugged his shoulders and gambled 6♠. Wouldn't you?

Moshe, West, led the ◊4. Declarer played low from dummy. East played the ◊5 and pleaded with declarer, "My five, please stay off it!"

"You think I'd let you win a cheap trick when I'm in slam?" said South. He won the ◊A and cashed the ♠A, catching the ♠9 from West and the ♣3 from East. When he continued with the ♠K, West's ♠10 fell and East threw a diamond.

South said to Moshe, "You sneaky devil! I'm onto you by now."

Then he turned to East and said, "You want to see a cheap trick?"

With that he led the ♠5, saying, "Now there's a 'high five' for you!"

South ran off the rest of his trumps, keeping only three clubs and the ♡A in dummy, but Moshe clung to all four of his clubs and scored the ♣Q and ♣9 at the end. Down one.

Was declarer any luckier in the other room?

Yes. There after West's tricky falsecards at Tricks 2 and 3, South, the Hellcat Hustler, exited with the ♠2. West won the ♠3 and shifted to the ♣2 at Trick 5. South won dummy's ♣J and threw her ◊3 on dummy's ♡A.

She said, "Not much help from you, partner, but I get by with a little help from my friends."

DEAL 86. MORE HELP TO GET TO DUMMY

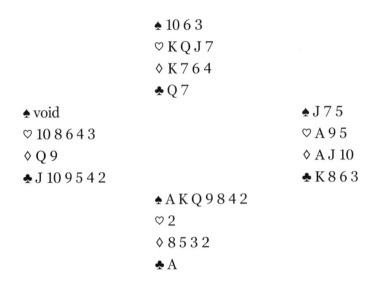

```
                    ♠ 10 6 3
                    ♡ K Q J 7
                    ◊ K 7 6 4
                    ♣ Q 7
    ♠ void                          ♠ J 7 5
    ♡ 10 8 6 4 3                    ♡ A 9 5
    ◊ Q 9                           ◊ A J 10
    ♣ J 10 9 5 4 2                  ♣ K 8 6 3
                    ♠ A K Q 9 8 4 2
                    ♡ 2
                    ◊ 8 5 3 2
                    ♣ A
```

East opened 1♣ in second seat, and West was unwilling to bid a vulnerable 5♣ over South's non-vul 4♠.

South won West's ♣J opening lead and drew trumps. He led to dummy's ♡J. East won the ♡A, South ruffed East's ♣K return. The diamond finesse lost (surprise!), so declarer came up a trick short.

Down one, minus 50.

Was there a better line for declarer?

Yes. In the other room, the bidding and play began the same, but when West showed out on the first trump, declarer didn't lead another. Instead, he led to dummy's ♡J.

East won the ♡A and led the ♣K, but South let him win it, discarding a diamond. Now the defenders could not stop declarer from reaching dummy to cash two heart tricks.

Making 4♠, plus 420.

DEAL 87. EVEN MORE HELP

```
                        ♠ Q J 2
                        ♡ A K J 2
                        ◊ 8 6 4 3
                        ♣ A 8
    ♠ 4                                      ♠ 8 7
    ♡ void                                   ♡ Q 10 9 8 7 6 4
    ◊ K Q 10 7 5                             ◊ J
    ♣ K Q J 10 9 7 5                         ♣ 6 4 3
                        ♠ A K 10 9 6 5 3
                        ♡ 5 3
    Roger               ◊ A 9 2
                        ♣ 2
```

East opened an emaciated "favorable vulnerability" 3♡ as dealer. South overcalled 3♠, West jumped to 5♣ as a "premature save" and North joined the jumpathon with 6♠.

Should West have sacrificed in 7♣? A case can be made both ways.

The IMP odds say yes, the probabilities say no. Especially when the contract may fail. Oops, did we say "the contract may fail"?

Sorry, contracts never make or fail; *players make, or fail in, them.*

West led the ♣K. Declarer won dummy's ♣A and ruffed a club. He drew trumps with the ♠Q and ♠K, then, playing for some kind of red-suit squeeze against East, he led the ◊2.

Did it work? Roger, Southwest, didn't say. When he reported this deal, Jim smiled and joked, "It'll work if East is 2=7=4=2."

Danny smiled more broadly and said, "Or 2=7=1=3 on a Crocodile Coup." Would West know what to play from ◊KQ1075 or ◊KJ1075?

In the Closed Room, declarer catered to East's 2=7=1=3 by cashing the ◊A and ducking a heart to East's ♡4. That definitely worked! East faced a Hobson's Choice. A second heart lets declarer discard two diamonds on dummy's hearts. A third club lets declarer discard a one diamond while ruffing in dummy and another diamond on dummy's hearts.

DEAL 88. ENTRIES TO BOTH HANDS

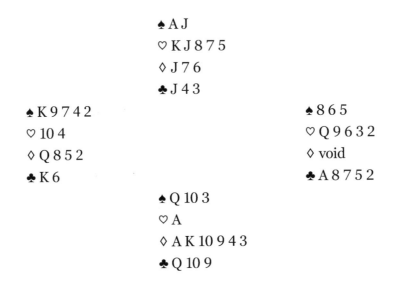

♠ A J
♡ K J 8 7 5
◊ J 7 6
♣ J 4 3

♠ K 9 7 4 2   ♠ 8 6 5
♡ 10 4   ♡ Q 9 6 3 2
◊ Q 8 5 2   ◊ void
♣ K 6   ♣ A 8 7 5 2

♠ Q 10 3
♡ A
◊ A K 10 9 4 3
♣ Q 10 9

West led the ♠4 against 3NT, and dummy's ♠J won. Declarer saw that if the ◊Q fell in the first two rounds, he had no shortage of tricks. But what if she didn't?

To ensure five diamonds and two tricks in each major if things went badly, South unblocked his ♡A at Trick 2, before dummy's last entry, the ♠A, could be dislodged.

Then South attacked diamonds, from which he needed only five tricks. He led the ◊A only to see East show out. When he continued with a low diamond to preserve an entry to his hand, West ducked. Now he had no hand entry left to score more than three diamond tricks and he wound up down two.

Any way to have avoided this disaster?

In the other room, a less greedy declarer unblocked the ♡A at Trick 2 and led low to dummy's ◊J next. West ducked the first diamond but won the second when South led to the ◊9. Soon declarer claimed her nine tricks.

"Very thoughtful play," said Danny, who was watching at her table.

"Thoughtful? Not at all," she demurred. "I don't sweat the overtricks at IMPs. I just saw the tricks I needed for my contract and went after them without worry about one- and two-IMP swings. That way, when I find myself in an iffy slam, I have energy left to give it my best effort."

DEAL 89. RINGO'S RULE AGAIN

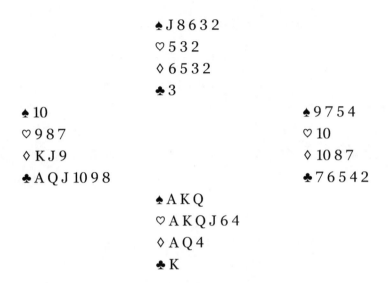

```
              ♠ J 8 6 3 2
              ♡ 5 3 2
              ◇ 6 5 3 2
              ♣ 3
♠ 10                          ♠ 9 7 5 4
♡ 9 8 7                       ♡ 10
◇ K J 9                       ◇ 10 8 7
♣ A Q J 10 9 8                ♣ 7 6 5 4 2
              ♠ A K Q
              ♡ A K Q J 6 4
              ◇ A Q 4
              ♣ K
```

West bravely bid 3♣ over South's strong, artificial and forcing 2♣. East raised to 5♣ obstructively. Undeterred, South pushed on to 5♡.

West led the ♣A. North spread the dummy and asked, "Will a jack be enough for you?" The ◇J would have been enough, but was the ♠J?

West shifted to the ♡9 at Trick 2. South won and cashed another top trump. East discarded the ◇7.

For once, a Red-on-Red Coup seemed to work. South drew no more trumps but started to run spades. On the second spade, West asked, "Did you forget about this little guy?" as he ruffed,

That was the end of the defense. South won West's diamond shift with the ◇Q, led low to dummy's ♡5, and threw the ◇4 on dummy's ♠J.

Was a successful defense possible?

In the other room, Moshe was West. Favorable vulnerability and an Omnibus 2♣ opening on his right are to him as a red flag is to a bull, so he jumped to 4♣. East bid 5♣ thinking it a no-ace reply as to Blackwood.

South, not to be shut out, took the push to 5♡.

The play started as in the Open Room, but when South left him with a trump, Moshe looked declarer in the eye and asked her, "Did you think you were Ringo Starr?" as he discarded a club.

South replied, "Yes, and I was hoping you were James Taylor," as she went peacefully down one.

DEAL 90. NO DUMMY ENTRY? GET SOME HELP

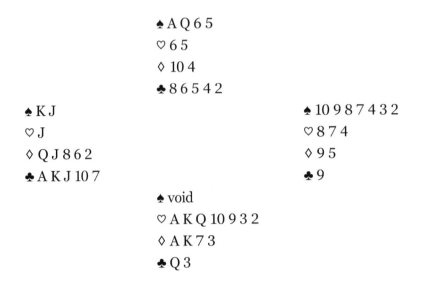

```
                    ♠ A Q 6 5
                    ♡ 6 5
                    ◊ 10 4
                    ♣ 8 6 5 4 2
♠ K J                                   ♠ 10 9 8 7 4 3 2
♡ J                                     ♡ 8 7 4
◊ Q J 8 6 2                             ◊ 9 5
♣ A K J 10 7                            ♣ 9
                    ♠ void
                    ♡ A K Q 10 9 3 2
                    ◊ A K 7 3
                    ♣ Q 3
```

The "Unusual Notrump Overcall" was probably Alvin Roth's greatest contribution to bridge, but it can boomerang when its users' minors are outranked by the opening side's majors. Then it may provide a blueprint for an opposing declarer.

On this deal, there was no stopping South from bidding 4♡.

West cashed two top clubs and continued with the ♣J. Declarer realized the futility of trying to cash and ruff diamonds. He ran off some extra trumps but lost two diamonds at the end to go with the two clubs he lost early. He went peacefully down one.

Could declarer have succeeded?

In the other room, South took advantage of the shape information West's 2NT had provided. After ruffing the third club with the ♡3, South cashed two top trumps before leading the ◊A and ◊K. When East followed to both, South exited with the ♡2.

East won and had to lead spades up to dummy's ♠AQ. 4♡ made.

DEAL 91. STEPPING STONES

```
                    ♠ J 8
                    ♡ A K 8 7 6
                    ◇ 7
                    ♣ A K 6 4 2
    ♠ 5 3                              ♠ A 6 2
    ♡ Q 4 3                            ♡ 10 9 5 2
    ◇ A K 10 9 8 5                     ◇ Q
    ♣ Q 10                             ♣ J 9 8 7 3
                    ♠ K Q 10 9 7 4
                    ♡ J
                    ◇ J 6 4 3 2
                    ♣ 5
```

We'll leave it to the reader to figure out how South became declarer in 4♠ after North opened 1♡ as dealer. West led the ◇A and switched to the ♠3 despite East's encouraging signal. East won the ♠A and returned the ♠2.

Declarer won and drew the last trump, guessing to discard a club from dummy and work on hearts, the stronger of dummy's two suits. He led the ♡J, captured West's ♡Q with dummy's ♡K, threw a diamond on dummy's ♡A and ruffed a heart.

Then he led to the ♣K and threw another diamond on dummy's ♣A. He led dummy's ♡7 and ruffed East's ♡10, but then he was stuck in his hand with ♠Q ◇J6. Dummy's ♡8 was stranded. Only nine tricks, minus 100.

Could South have rescued dummy's lonely fifth heart?

In the other room. South did. The play to the first eight tricks was the same, but when dummy was on lead in the five-card ending …

```
North: ♠none   ♡87   ◇none   ♣A64
                              East: ♠none   ♡10   ◇none   ♣KJ87
South: ♠Q10   ♡none   ◇J64   ♣none
```

… declarer threw the ◇4 on dummy's ♡7, letting East win his now-bare ♡10. With only ♣J987 left, East had to put dummy in. Two more discards on dummy's ♣A and ♡8 meant 10 tricks, plus 620.

DEAL 92. STEPPING STONES WORK BOTH WAYS

```
                    ♠ 10 7 6 3 2
                    ♡ 9 6 4
                    ◊ A K Q
                    ♣ A 6
♠ A K Q 9 8 4                              ♠ void
♡ 7 5 3 2                                  ♡ 8
◊ 7                                        ◊ 10 9 8 6 4
♣ 10 4                                     ♣ K J 9 8 7 5 2
                    ♠ J 5
                    ♡ A K Q J 10
                    ◊ J 5 3 2
                    ♣ Q 3
```

West opened a Weak 2♠ Bid as dealer on adverse vulnerability. South bid 3♡ when this came round to him, and North raised to 4♡.

West led the ♠K, promising the ♠Q, and then the ♠A. Ignoring East's high-low club discards, he continued with the ♠9. East's ♡8 "uppercut" didn't promote a trump trick for West, but it did shorten South's trumps.

South used all his trumps to draw West's four low ones. He discarded a spade from dummy while East discarded low diamonds. After unblocking dummy's diamonds, declarer remained with ◊J ♣Q3 while dummy had ♠7 ♣A6. Dummy's ♣A was declarer's ninth trick and his last. Down one.

Whose fault?

South was wrong. North's ♣A had become a liability instead of an asset. Had South discarded it on the last trump, this would be the ending:

North: ♠76 ♡none ◊none ♣6

East: ♠none ♡none ◊10 ♣K8
or
East: ♠none ♡none ◊109 ♣K

South: ♠none ♡none ◊J ♣Q3

Then declarer could lead dummy's ♣6 to score two of the last three tricks and make 4♡ regardless which three cards East kept.

North was wrong too. In the other room, North bid 3NT, the easy game, instead of 4♡, the hard one.

DEAL 93. CREATE A STEPPING STONE TO DUMMY

```
                        ♠ Q 10 5
                        ♡ 5 3
                        ◊ 8 7 4 2
                        ♣ K Q 6 3
        ♠ J 8 6 3 2                          ♠ 9 4
        ♡ 9 8 4                              ♡ J 7
        ◊ 9                                  ◊ A Q J 10
        ♣ A J 9 5                            ♣ 10 8 7 4 2
                        ♠ A K 7
                        ♡ A K Q 10 6 2
                        ◊ K 6 5 3            Danny
                        ♣ void
```

On Board 8, South opened 1♡ in fourth seat and jumped to 4♡ over North's 1NT response. 3NT is better, but who could know without peeking?

West led his singleton ◊9 to East's ◊A and ruffed declarer's ◊K at Trick 2. West's passive trump exit left declarer with two diamond losers.

South finished drawing trump and crossed to dummy's ♠Q to try a ruffing finesse in clubs. He discarded a diamond on dummy's ♣K. West won the ♣A and exited in spades. As dummy had no entry left, dummy's ♣Q rotted on the vine. Down one.

Danny caddied Boards 5 to 8 to the other room, where Stella and Moshe opposed each other. He stayed to see those boards played again.

On Board 8, Moshe received the same defense in 4♡ and winked at Danny as he stuck his ♠A between his two remaining diamonds. He drew trump, unblocked the ♠K and finessed dummy's ♠10. When it won, he led dummy's ♣K and discarded the ♠A, leaving:

```
        Stella by Starlight              North: ♠Q   ♡none   ◊87   ♣Q63
West: ♠J86   ♡none   ◊none   ♣AJ9
                                         South: ♠none   ♡Q1062   ◊65   ♣none
```

If West won the ♣A, South would throw diamonds on North's black queens. Stella flung her cards face down on the table, conceded 4♡ and muttered "Lucky, lucky!"

"Moshe reads Frank Stewart's columns too, Stella," said Danny.

Yes, Frank had shown this theme in his entertaining and instructive newspaper column.

DEAL 94. A STEPPING STONE ENTRY TO DUMMY

```
                          ♠ 5
                          ♡ Q J 5 4
                          ◊ 8 7 5 4
                          ♣ K 6 4 3
        ♠ Q               ♠ 9 6 4 3
        ♡ 9 6                              ♡ 10 8 7 3 2
        ◊ A K J 9 6 3 2                    ◊ Q
        ♣ Q 10 9                           ♣ A 8 7
                          ♠ A K J 10 8 7 2
                          ♡ A K
                          ◊ 10
                          ♣ J 5 2
```

East responded 1♡ to West's 1◊ opening and South's 4♠ bought the contract. Declarer ruffed the second diamond and drew trump, discarding two diamonds and a club from dummy. Then he unblocked the ♡AK and tried to reach dummy with a club. He lost three club tricks. Down one.

Was there a way to reach dummy to cash two more heart tricks?

In the other room, the Hellcat Hustler declared 4♠. She took care to ruff the second diamond with the ♠7 and drew only three rounds of trumps. After unblocking her hearts, she led the ♠2 in this position:

North: ♠none   ♡QJ   ◊8   ♣K64

East: ♠3   ♡108   ◊none   ♣A87   *(Moshe)*

South: ♠1082   ♡none   ◊none   ♣J62

Moshe, East, shook a finger at HH and said, "Shame on you, girl! Didn't you attend my class on Drawing Trump? I'm afraid I must flunk you."

With that he won the ♠3, cashed the ♣A and slipped the rest of his cards into the duplicate rack. Having only hearts and clubs left he would have been forced to put dummy in. He muttered "Naughty, naughty girl," as he marked minus 420 on his scorecard.

DEAL 95. ANOTHER STEPPING STONE ENTRY TO DUMMY

                            ♠ Q J 10 8
                            ♡ J 4
                            ♢ J 9 7 6 4
Moshe   ♣ Q 3
♠ 7 6 4   ♠ K 5 3
♡ 2   ♡ Q 10 9 8 7 3
♢ 5 3   ♢ 8 2
♣ K J 10 9 7 6 2   ♣ 8 5
                            ♠ A 9 2
                            ♡ A K 6 5
                            ♢ A K Q 10
                            ♣ A 4

Favorable vulnerability spurred West to preempt 4♣ over South's Omnibus 2♣ opening. Very frustrating to South, who had planned a nice quiet "Kokish" 2♡relay followed by 2NT to describe his big balanced hand. When 4♣ rolled around to him, he bid 4NT to play. Confusion everywhere!

North bid 5♣. Stayman? Reply to Blackwood? Or an old-fashioned cue bid? Thinking it Stayman, South bid 5♡. Bewildered, North bid 5NT. Equally bewildered, South bid 6NT and mumbled, "Sheep for a lamb!"

West led the ♢5. South counted 11 tricks if the ♠K were onside guarded twice or thrice. A twelfth trick could come if West held the ♡Q. He won the ♢A and led low to dummy's ♡J. East won and exited the ♣8. South rose ♣A and ran diamonds, discarding the ♣4. He floated dummy's quacks; East ducked twice. In the end, he lost a second heart trick to East. Down one.

Could South have made 6NT?

Yes. Run the diamonds, pitching the ♣A. Three rounds of spades, finessing. Take two top hearts. That's 10 tricks, leaving:

                            North: ♠10 ♡none ♢none ♣Q3
West: ♠none ♡none ♢none ♣KJ10
                            South: ♠none ♡65 ♢none ♣4

The ♣4 towards dummy's remaining ♠10 ♣Q3 yields two more, as West has only ♣KJ10 left. That's 12 tricks.

In the other room, gentler invention by West, 3♣, led eventually to South declaring the easier 6♢ and an easy overtrick.

DEAL 96. YET ANOTHER STEPPING STONE ENTRY TO DUMMY

♠ Q 10 2
♡ 8 4 3
◇ 8 7 4 2
♣ Q J 3

♠ 7 6 4 3   ♠ 9 8 5
♡ 10 7 6 2   ♡ 9
◇ Q   ◇ A J 10 9
♣ K 9 7 6   ♣ 10 8 5 4 2

♠ A K J
♡ A K Q J 5
◇ K 6 5 3
♣ A

We'd want to play in 3NT, wouldn't you? We'd bid it with North's hand after South shows a powerhouse with five hearts and four diamonds.

However, the rest of the world persists in treating three low trumps without a ruffing value as "support," and so South landed in the 4♡ swamp.

West led the ◇Q to East's ◇A and ruffed off declarer's ◇K at Trick 2. South won West's trump exit and drew trumps. He cashed the ♣A and three spades ending in dummy, then tried a ruffing finesse in clubs, discarding a diamond on dummy's ♣Q. West won the ♣K and led the ♠7.

South ruffed, but lost another diamond at Trick 13. He cried, "Thirteen is an unlucky number. Why doesn't somebody invent a game with only twelve tricks?" as he marked minus 100 on his scorecard.

Could declarer have made better use of dummy's assets?

In the other room, declaring the same lame 4♡ game, South began the same way, but after finishing trumps he cashed the ♠A, overtook the ♠J with dummy's ♠Q, and discarded the ♠K on dummy's ♣Q next, leaving:

North: ♠10 ♡none ◇87 ♣J

West: ♠76 ♡none ◇none ♣97

South: ♠none ♡J5 ◇65 ♣none

West had to lead to dummy's winners. You've seen this play before, haven't you? We hope you don't have to see it 13 times to get it right.

DEAL 97. A STEPPING STONE TO
CREATE A DUMMY ENTRY

♠ 4 3 2
♡ A Q J
♢ Q J 7 6 4
♣ K Q

♠ K 8 7   ♠ 5
♡ 10 9 8 6 4   ♡ 7 5 3 2
♢ 3   ♢ K 10 9
♣ J 4 3 2   ♣ 10 8 7 6 5

♠ A Q J 10 9 6
♡ K
♢ A 8 5 2
♣ A 9

After discovering the double fit, South did well to bid 6♠ rather than 6♢. The possible 2-IMP gain if both make meant little, but the lower solidity of the spades meant a lot. Too many otherwise good slams fail when a defender scores a missing jack or ten of trumps.

West led the ♡10. South won dummy's ♡A to finesse the ♠Q. West did well to play the ♠8 in tempo, hoping South might fear it were singleton and burn a dummy entry to finesse again.

Sure enough, South crossed to dummy's ♣K to lead the ♠3. When East showed out, he won the ♠A. Bereft of dummy entries, he lost to both missing kings, the ♠K and the ♢K. Down one.

Could South have found an extra dummy entry to finesse diamonds?

Yes, with a little help from his friends and a little extra precaution on his own part. In the other room, South took that precaution in 6♠. Tricks 1, 2 and 3 were the same. At Trick 4, however, before leading dummy's second spade, he discarded his ♣A on dummy's ♡J. When East showed out on the second spade, South played the ♠A and then the ♠J to West's ♠K, leaving:

West: ♠none   ♡986   ♢3   ♣J43

North: ♠none   ♡Q   ♢QJ764   ♣Q

South: ♠1096   ♡none   ♢A852   ♣none

West had no spades left. He had to lead to dummy's Amazonian queens. Christmas! North sang, "We three queens of orient are." 6♠ made.

CAREFULLY

PRESERVED

DEAL 98. PERFECT PATTI GETS HER NAME IN THE BOOK

```
                        ♠ A Q J 10
                        ♡ A
                        ◊ 10 9 4 2
                        ♣ Q J 10 4
     ♠ K 9 6 2                              ♠ 7 3
     ♡ Q J 10 5                             ♡ K 9 7 4 2
     ◊ 8 7 6 3                              ◊ A 5
     ♣ 3            Patti                    ♣ 9 7 6 5
                        ♠ 8 5 4
                        ♡ 9 6 3
                        ◊ K Q J          Danny
                        ♣ A K 8 2
```

West led the ♡Q against Perfect Patti's 3NT. Her potential diamond tricks went down the drain, as the defenders would cash the setting tricks in hearts. Her brown eyes lit up. She slapped her kibitzer and said, "Come on, Danny, watch. After I play this contract, I want you to put me in your book with Jim, and oh yes, you can sing to me *Beautiful, Beautiful Brown Eyes.*"

Patti overtook dummy's ♣Q with her ♣K. Then she finessed dummy's ♠10. Next she overtook dummy's ♣J with her ♣A. West discarded a diamond. A second spade finesse worked, but now she was at the end of her rope. Resignedly, she switched to diamonds. East won the ◊A, returned a low heart, and Patti lost four heart tricks. Down one.

Danny said, "All right, Patti, you'll go in the book on Entries," but the song he sang was *Weep You No More, Sad Fountains.*

Had Danny forgotten the tune to *Beautiful, Beautiful Brown Eyes?*

No. In the other room, Careful Kate received the same lead against 3NT but she was wide awake. She followed to dummy's ♣Q with the ♣2 at Trick 2. Only at Trick 3 did she overtake dummy's ♣J with her ♣K. When West showed out, she was able to finesse spades three times *and clubs once* to make her contract.

Jim, who was kibitzing Kate, whispered to her, "You're lucky Rose wasn't sitting on your right, She'd have played the nine on the third round of clubs to block the suit." Kate only smiled in reply.

DEAL 99. TRUMP ENTRIES: SPOT CARDS

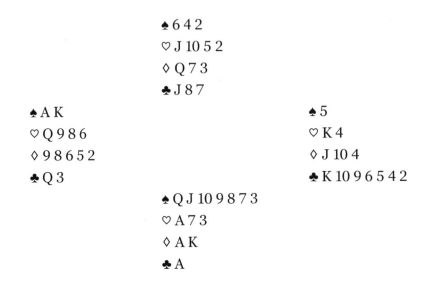

```
                        ♠ 6 4 2
                        ♡ J 10 5 2
                        ◇ Q 7 3
                        ♣ J 8 7
        ♠ A K                            ♠ 5
        ♡ Q 9 8 6                        ♡ K 4
        ◇ 9 8 6 5 2                      ◇ J 10 4
        ♣ Q 3                            ♣ K 10 9 6 5 4 2
                        ♠ Q J 10 9 8 7 3
                        ♡ A 7 3
                        ◇ A K
                        ♣ A
```

East's "third seat, favorable vulnerability" 3♣ didn't keep South from bidding 4♠.

West led the ♣Q to declarer's ♣A. South led the ♠Q to start to draw trumps. West took his two top spades before leading his last club.

South ruffed and needed seven of the nine remaining tricks. He unblocked both diamonds but had no way to avoid losing two heart tricks from here.

"Partner, didn't we just discuss this very situation?" asked North as he marked minus 100 on his scorecard and tried to hold back his tears.

How would a more perceptive declarer have played?

In the other room, where declarer faced the same challenges, she took care to follow to the second spade with the ♠7 and ruff the second club with the ♠8. Then, after unblocking diamonds, she led the ♠3 to dummy's ♠6 and discarded a heart on the ◇Q.

At this table, North smiled silently marking plus 620 on his scorecard.

DEAL 100. SAVING YOUR DUMMY ENTRY

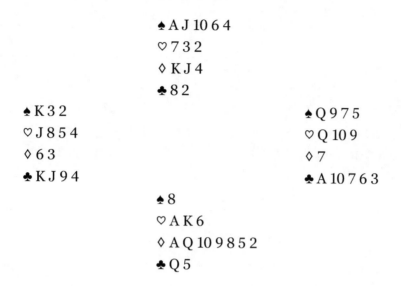

```
                  ♠ A J 10 6 4
                  ♡ 7 3 2
                  ◊ K J 4
                  ♣ 8 2
   ♠ K 3 2                        ♠ Q 9 7 5
   ♡ J 8 5 4                      ♡ Q 10 9
   ◊ 6 3                          ◊ 7
   ♣ K J 9 4                      ♣ A 10 7 6 3
                  ♠ 8
                  ♡ A K 6
                  ◊ A Q 10 9 8 5 2
                  ♣ Q 5
```

North and South did well to avoid a 3NT contract that could be beaten off the top and landed in 5◊.

The defense began with the ♣4 to the ♣A and the ♣6 back to the ♣K. West shifted to the ♡4, and South captured East's ♡Q with the ♡A.

How can South avoid a heart loser? We'll let you take over from here.

Spades offer the only hope. A 4-3 split, or a lucky fall of a doubleton monarch in the West hand or a ♠KQ in the East hand, will let you set up a second spade trick in dummy. Trumps will serve as entries.

So, a spade to the ♠A and ruff a spade. Trump to dummy's ◊J (thank heaven both defenders follow!) and ruff another spade (thank heaven both follow again). Lead another trump to dummy's ◊K and ruff another spade.
Cross to dummy with a third trump and discard your low heart on dummy's established ♠J.

What? You don't have the ◊2 left in your hand? What did we tell you earlier about the care and feeding of deuces?

DEAL 101. TRUMP ENTRIES: SPOT CARDS

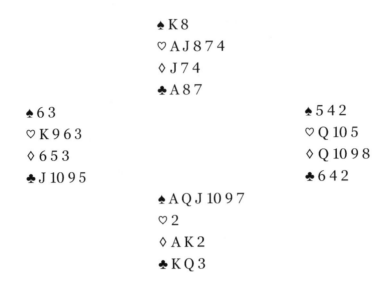

```
                    ♠ K 8
                    ♡ A J 8 7 4
                    ◊ J 7 4
                    ♣ A 8 7
    ♠ 6 3                              ♠ 5 4 2
    ♡ K 9 6 3                          ♡ Q 10 5
    ◊ 6 5 3                            ◊ Q 10 9 8
    ♣ J 10 9 5                         ♣ 6 4 2
                    ♠ A Q J 10 9 7
                    ♡ 2
                    ◊ A K 2
                    ♣ K Q 3
```

North opened 1♡. South jumped to 2♠ and later used Roman Keycard Blackwood adroitly to reach 7♠. If only North had a genuine diamond stopper, the ◊Q instead of the nearly useless ◊J, 7♠ would be a lock!

West led the ♣J. South won the ♣K and went about ruffing out the hearts. Heart to the ♡A, heart ruff, spade to the ♠K, another heart ruff. East's ♡Q fell on the third heart but the ♡K was still out.

Declarer drew trumps, which split 3-2, and crossed to dummy's ♣A to ruff out the ♡K with his last trump. But he had no dummy entry left to cash the ♡J. When the ◊Q didn't fall on the first two rounds, 7♠ went down.

How did the declarer in the other room make it?

In the other room, South took his first ruff with the ♠9 and led the ♠7 to dummy's ♠8 to ruff another heart with an honor. Then he led to dummy's ♠K to ruff a third heart, drew the last trump discarding a diamond from dummy, and claimed the rest.

Little things mean a lot, especially in bridge. One declarer failed to appreciate the *♠8 and the lower spade he could have led to it*. The other declarer appreciated both, and played accordingly.

DEAL 102. TRUMP ENTRIES: SPOT CARDS

```
                    ♠ A K 3
                    ♡ 7 2
                    ◊ 8 6 5
                    ♣ A Q J 8 4
♠ Q 8 4                              ♠ 10 9
♡ A Q 10 6                           ♡ J 9 8 4
◊ Q J 3                              ◊ K 7 4 2
♣ 10 6 2                             ♣ 9 5 3
                    ♠ J 7 6 5 2
                    ♡ K 5 3
                    ◊ A 10 9
                    ♣ K 7
```

South responded 1♠ to North's 1♣. North raised to 2♠ and carried on to 4♠ when South bid 3♠ to show a fifth spade and invite game.

South ducked West's ◊Q opening lead and won her ◊J continuation. He cashed dummy's two top trumps, catching only low trumps from the defenders. Three rounds of clubs provided a diamond discard, and a fourth club let declarer discard a heart.

West ruffed the fourth club with the master trump and led her last diamond. Declarer trumped, but with the ♠J7 and ♡K5 remaining, he had to lead hearts from his hand. He lost two hearts in addition to the spade and diamond already lost. Down one.

In the other room, the play in 4♠ was almost identical, but with one small difference that enabled declarer to make 4♠.

What was that small difference?

The declarer in the other room took care to preserve her ♠2, so that her last four cards were ♠J2 and ♡K5. At Trick 10, she led the ♠2 to dummy's ♠3. Then she discarded the ♡5 on dummy's last club to avoid a second heart loser. Making 4♠.

DEAL 103. FINDING THAT ELUSIVE DUMMY ENTRY

```
                    ♠ A K 9 7 3
                    ♡ 8 7 3
                    ◊ 10 6 4
                    ♣ Q J
      ♠ 8 4                            ♠ Q J 10 6
      ♡ 6 4                            ♡ A 5
      ◊ K J 7 3                        ◊ 8 5 2
      ♣ K 10 7 5 3                     ♣ 9 8 6 4
                    ♠ 5 2
                    ♡ K Q J 10 9 2
                    ◊ A Q 9
                    ♣ A 2
```

West led a passive ♡4 against 4♡. East won the ♡A as South followed low. East shifted to the ◊8, ducked to West's ◊J. West continued his passive defense with another trump.

Declarer won and ducked a spade, hoping for a 3-3 split to see him home. East won and continued with the ◊5. South won the ◊A and led to dummy's ♠K. He discarded the ◊Q on dummy's ♠A.

When spades failed to split 3-3, declarer tried a club finesse. West's ♣K took the setting trick.

Do you see how declarer could have made 4♡?

In the other room, play began similarly but with one tiny exception. There South preserved her ♡2. After she ducked a spade to East, she won his diamond continuation with the ◊A, cashed dummy's two top spades to discard the ◊Q, and ruffed a spade high to establish dummy's fifth spade.

Then she led the ♡2 to dummy and discarded the ♣2 on dummy's fifth spade. Making 4♡, with one trick lost in every suit but clubs.

DEAL 104. AN EASY DUMMY ENTRY
IF YOU'RE CAREFUL

```
                    ♠ A Q J 5
                    ♡ 6 4 2
                    ◇ 8 7 6
                    ♣ 9 7 2
      ♠ 7 3                          ♠ K 10 9 8 6 4
      ♡ A 7                          ♡ 8 3
      ◇ A J 2                        ◇ 10 5 4 3
      ♣ Q J 10 6 5 4                 ♣ K
                    ♠ 2
                    ♡ K Q J 10 9 5
                    ◇ K Q 9
                    ♣ A 8 3
```

West opened 1♣ and remained silent after East responded 1♠ and South overcalled 2♡. East balanced with 2♠, pushing South to 3♡.

West's ♣Q opening lead went to East's ♣K and South's ♣A. West captured South's ♡K at Trick 2, cashed two club tricks and exited in trump.

South slipped the ◇Q past West, and then ran off some trump tricks. West saved the ◇AJ till the end to take the setting tricks.

Do you see how to take nine tricks?

In the other room, the other South visualized nine tricks clearly: five trump tricks, two minor-suit aces, and two or three spade tricks (depending on the location of the ♠K).

Once he saw trumps split 2-2, the other declarer led to dummy's ♠A and took a ruffing spade finesse. East covered dummy's ♠Q with the ♠K but declarer ruffed high.

Then he led his carefully-preserved ♡5 to dummy's ♡6 and discarded the ◇9 on dummy's ♠J,

DEAL 105. CAREFULLY PRESERVED
IS CAREFULLY PRESERVED

♠ A 7 4 3
♡ 9 7 4
◊ 8 3
♣ A 7 4 2

♠ 5 2
♡ A K Q J 10 8 6
◊ K 6 2
♣ 6

♠ K J
♡ 5 3
◊ Q J 10 7 4
♣ J 10 8 3

♠ Q 10 9 8 6
♡ 2
◊ A 9 5
♣ K Q 9 5

As usual when it's hearts versus spades, the spades bought the contract. After South opened 1♠ and West gambled 4♡, North bid 4♠ not knowing whether to make or save.

South ruffed the second heart. He led to dummy's ♠A and surrendered a trick to East's ♠K. Declarer ducked East's ◊Q shift, won the next diamond and ruffed his last diamond in dummy.

By now, South could read West's hand-pattern as either 2=7=3=1 or 2=7=4=0. Declarer led the ♣5 to dummy's ♣A and the ♣2 back. East split his honors, and South captured his ♣10 with the ♣Q. Alas, he had no way back to dummy for another club finesse. Down one.

"It's all right, partner," said South. "They can make four hearts."

Was it really all right?

Eddie Kantar introduced the phrase "carefully-preserved deuce" to our bridge lexicon, but any card low enough to serve as an entry to partner's hand deserves the epithet. So get in the habit of looking fondly upon such cards.

Low trumps can be squandered almost as easily as high ones. In the other room, South took care to preserve his ♠6, which he overtook with dummy's carefully-preserved ♠7 to take a third-round finesse through East's remaining ♣J8. He made 4♠.

PART TWO

THE DEFENSE

Chapter 7. Dislodging Dummy's Entry

DEAL 106. KILL DUMMY'S ENTRY; REMEMBER THE BIDDING

```
                      ♠ Q 9
                      ♡ A Q 8 4 3 2
                      ◇ 8 7 2
                      ♣ 9 5
     ♠ 10 8 6 3 2                     ♠ A K 7 5
     ♡ J 10 7                         ♡ K 9 6
     ◇ 10                             ◇ J 6 4 3
     ♣ 8 7 4 2                        ♣ J 3
                      ♠ J 4
                      ♡ 5
                      ◇ A K Q 9 5
                      ♣ A K Q 10 6
```

South dealt and opened 1◇, then forced to game with a 3♣ jump over North's 1♡ response. North rebid 3♡ and took a 4◇ preference over South's 4♣ rebid. South's 5◇ ended the auction.

West led the ♠3 to East's ♠K and followed to East's ♠A with the ♠2.

Declarer won East's ♣J shift with the ♣A and cashed the ◇AK, learning of the 1-4 trump split. So he crossed to dummy's ♡A, picked up East's trumps with a proven finesse, crossed to dummy's ♣9 and claimed the rest.

Making 5◇.

How did the defenders beat 5◇ in the other room?

After winning the first two spades, East reflected upon the bidding. Having turned up with two spades and shown at least 5-5 in the minors, South could have no more than one heart. That heart could be an entry to dummy.

Declarer could use it to reach dummy for a diamond finesse after discovering the unfavorable trump split. So East led a heart before South knew of how trumps were divided.

Declarer won dummy's ♡Q but then he had no dummy entry to finesse East's ◇J. Down one.

112

DEAL 107. THE KAMIKAZE COUP

```
                    ♠ A K 7 4
                    ♡ 8 6
                    ◇ A Q 4 3 2
                    ♣ 9 6
    ♠ Q 10 6 2                      ♠ J 9 8
    ♡ K Q 10 9 3                    ♡ 5 4 2
    ◇ K 9                          ◇ 10 8 7 5
    ♣ 4 3                          ♣ A 7 5
                    ♠ 5 3
                    ♡ A J 7
                    ◇ J 6
                    ♣ K Q J 10 8 2
```

West's 1♡ overcall did not keep his opponents from reaching game. After North responded 2◇ and rebid 3♠ over 3♣, South bid 3NT.

Back in the 1950s, Danny used to lead the queen from suits headed by KQ109. Ostensibly, this showed the jack, but Danny trusted his young partners to figure out to drop the jack if they knew he didn't have it.

Now that this kind of queen-lead is standard practice, West led the ♡Q. East played the ♡2, denying the ♡J and showing count. South ducked.

Nonetheless West continued with the ♡K to declarer's ♡A. South led the ♣2 to dummy's ♣9. East won the ♣A and returned his last heart. Declarer won the ♡J, ran clubs and romped home with 10 tricks.

East was unhappy. "Why did you throw your king of hearts under the bus? Didn't you read the account of the woman in South Bend who threw her four-year-old son in front a Greyhound Scenicruiser in 1957?"

"No," admitted West. "But didn't you read how much damage those Japanese kamikaze pilots inflicted more than a dozen years before that?"

Who was right, the bus driver or the kamikaze pilot?

Oops, wrong question. West was right. His sequence of plays showed ♡KQ109 without the ♡J. East must duck the first club, win the second, and lead diamonds specifically to prevent a throw-in. Then South can never reach his hand to run clubs, and 3NT will fail.

West's play was a Kamikaze Coup to counter South's Bath Coup.

DEAL 108. REMOVING DUMMY'S ENTRY

```
                        ♠ 9 7 6
                        ♡ 10 9 6 3
                        ◇ A Q 4
                        ♣ 8 7 4
        ♠ 10 8 3 2                       ♠ A 5 4
        ♡ A J 4                          ♡ 8 7 5 2
        ◇ K 8 5 2                        ◇ J 10
        ♣ 9 2                            ♣ J 10 6 5
                        ♠ K Q J
                        ♡ K Q
                        ◇ 9 7 6 3
                        ♣ A K Q 4
```

North raised South's 20-21 HCP 2NT opening to 3NT. He wisely eschewed Stayman with a flat hand and a weak four-card major.

West led the ♠2. East won the ♠A and South dropped the ♠K.

"You can't fool me," said East as he returned the ♠5. "I know you wouldn't do that without the queen."

"You're right," smiled South sheepishly as he won the ♠Q. Next he led the ♡K. West won the ♡A to clear the spades. Upon winning the ♠J, South unblocked the ♡Q, finessed the ◇Q successfully, and drove out West's ♡J.

The defenders won two hearts and two spades, but that was all. Declarer limped home with three club tricks and two tricks in every other suit.

Could the defenders have beaten 3NT? Which defender was to blame for letting it make?

Both.

East might have realized at Trick 1 that spades offered little hope. Knowing that none of his hearts could beat dummy's on the third or fourth round, East might have shifted to the ◇J in hope of killing an entry to dummy's hearts.

West might have led the ◇2, or a "second highest from length and strength" ♠8 (making things clearer for his partner) at Trick 1.

DEAL 109. REMOVING DUMMY'S ENTRIES

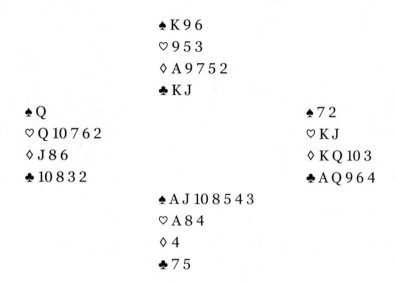

♠ K 9 6
♡ 9 5 3
◊ A 9 7 5 2
♣ K J

♠ Q
♡ Q 10 7 6 2
◊ J 8 6
♣ 10 8 3 2

♠ 7 2
♡ K J
◊ K Q 10 3
♣ A Q 9 6 4

♠ A J 10 8 5 4 3
♡ A 8 4
◊ 4
♣ 7 5

East opened 1♣ in third seat, not everyone's choice, South overcalled 1♠ and jumped to 4♠ over North's 2NT advance.

West led the ♣2. East won the ♣Q and cashed the ♣A. West played the ♣8 hoping East would read it as preference for a heart shift. East obliged.

South captured East's ♡K with the ♡A and got to work on dummy's long suit. ◊A, diamond ruff with the ♠10, ♠3 to dummy's ♠K, diamond ruff with the ♠J, ♠8 to dummy's ♠9, diamond ruff low, and then the ♠4 to dummy's ♠6. Dummy's fifth diamond provided a tenth trick. Making 4♠.

Could the defenders have held declarer to nine tricks?

Yes. Just as one of declarer's best game plans is often to set up a long suit in dummy, a defender should recognize the danger that a long suit in dummy presents. So a defender's best game plan is often to attack dummy's outside entries. Here those entries were all in trump.

Look what a trump shift at Trick 3 does! Removing even only one trump entry to dummy foils declarer's game plan. Declarer comes up one trick short.

DEAL 110. REMOVING THE ENTRY FROM DUMMY

```
                        ♠ Q 4
                        ♡ Q 5 4
                        ◊ J 10 8 7 6
                        ♣ Q 9 8
        ♠ K 5 2                             ♠ void
        ♡ A K 10 9                          ♡ 8 7 6 2
        ◊ Q 9 3                             ◊ 5 2
        ♣ A J 6                             ♣ K 10 7 5 4 3 2
                        ♠ A J 10 9 8 7 6 3
                        ♡ J 3
                        ◊ A K 4
                        ♣ void
```

West opened 1NT and East responded 2♠, which they played as a transfer to clubs. South put his opponents to the test by bidding 4♠, but they neither doubled nor sacrificed.

Playing Patriarch Opening Leads, West led the ♡A and switched to the ♣A. South ruffed and led the ♡J, West won the ♡K, but now dummy's ♡Q was high and dummy's ♠Q was an entry to it. Away went declarer's low diamond, All declarer lost were the two top hearts and the ♠K. Making 4♠.

Could the defenders have beaten 4♠?

Yes, had West seen the danger posed by dummy's queens. The ♣A, if it were cashing, could wait. Killing dummy's entry (the ♠Q) could not wait.
At Trick 2, West should have shifted to the ♠5. Then declarer could use dummy's ♠Q before it would do him any good, or not at all.

In the other room, South reached 4♠ after a slightly different auction. West found the killings ♠5 shift at Trick 2. Dummy's ♠Q won, but declarer had to lose to West's ♠K, ♡K and ◊Q later. Down one.

DEAL 111. TRUMP RETURN TO REMOVE AN ENTRY

```
                        ♠ 8 5 2
                        ♡ K 9 5
                        ◊ K 8
                        ♣ A J 8 5 2
        ♠ K J 7 6                       ♠ Q 10 3
        ♡ 8                             ♡ 7 4
        ◊ 10 9 7 5 3                    ◊ A Q 6 2
        ♣ 7 4 3                         ♣ K Q 10 6
                        ♠ A 9 4
                        ♡ A Q J 10 6 3 2
                        ◊ J 4
                        ♣ 9
```

After East opened 1◊, South reached 4♡. West led the ◊10 and East won the first two tricks with diamond honors. Then he shifted to spades.

South won the ♠A to work on clubs. ♣A, club ruff with the ♡10, ♡6 to dummy's ♡5, club ruff with the ♡J, ♡Q to dummy's ♡K, and a third club ruff with the ♡A. Then the ♡2 to dummy's ♡5, and now the ♣J provided a discard for a spade loser. Declarer made 4♡ with seven heart tricks, both black aces, and dummy's ♣J.

"Didn't we just have another deal like this, partner?" lamented West. "How many times before you get it right?"

To what was West referring?

Timing. In the other room, East recognized the danger in dummy's long clubs and set about promptly to kill the entries that declarer needed to set up a long club in dummy. He shifted to the ♡4 at Trick 3.

One of dummy's three trump entries died an early death, having been consumed before it could be put to good use. The remaining two trump entries were one too few.

4♡ went down one.

"Good shift, partner," said West. "Reminds me of the defense that Cleveland Indians player-manager Lou Boudreau devised against Red Sox slugger Ted Williams."

DEAL 112. CHOOSE THE BATTLE YOU ARE SURE TO WIN

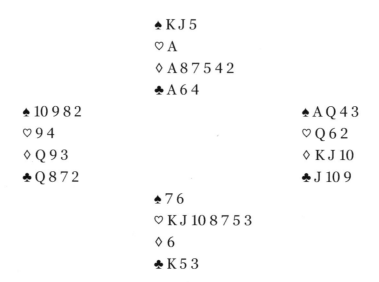

                    ♠ K J 5
                    ♡ A
                    ◇ A 8 7 5 4 2
                    ♣ A 6 4
    ♠ 10 9 8 2   ♠ A Q 4 3
    ♡ 9 4   ♡ Q 6 2
    ◇ Q 9 3   ◇ K J 10
    ♣ Q 8 7 2   ♣ J 10 9
                    ♠ 7 6
                    ♡ K J 10 8 7 5 3
                    ◇ 6
                    ♣ K 5 3

Vul against not, South feared to open 3♡ with so many losers. She opened a Weak 2♡ Bid instead. North did well to bid 4♡.

West led the ♠10 to dummy's ♠J and East's ♠Q. Declarer won East's ♣J shift with the ♣K and started diamonds: ◇A, diamond covered with East's ◇K and ruffed with the ♡7, ♡3 to dummy's ♡A, and a diamond ruff with the ♡8. South sighed with relief when the last outstanding diamonds fell together.

Now South cashed the ♡K and led the ♡J to East's ♡Q. East cashed the ♠A to stop an overtrick, but declarer ruffed the next spade, crossed to dummy's ♣A and threw the ♣5 on dummy's ◇5.

North and South exchanged "High fives" as each marked +620 on his scorecard.

Was stopping an overtrick the best that East could do?

In the other room, where North raised South's 3♡ opening to 4♡, East had an acute attack of longsuitophobia. She captured dummy's ♠J with her ♠Q at Trick 1 and realized she needed to attack dummy's entries promptly.

If West had the ♣K, a club shift would work wonders, but what if his club honor were the ♣Q? So East attacked the dummy entry she *knew she could dislodge*. Her trump shift left declarer one dummy entry short.

Eventually, the defenders set up and scored the setting trick in clubs.

DEAL 113. A CARD FALLS FROM A DEFENDER'S HAND

```
                    ♠ A 5
                    ♡ 7 5
                    ◊ 9 2
                    ♣ K J 10 9 8 7 3
    ♠ 9 8 6                           ♠ K 10 4 3 2
    ♡ J 10 8 2                        ♡ 9 6 4 3
    ◊ A 10 8 4                        ◊ Q 7
    ♣ 5 2                             ♣ A Q
                    ♠ Q J 7
                    ♡ A K Q
                    ◊ K J 6 5 3
                    ♣ 6 4
```

North raised South's 1NT opening to 3NT directly. He felt no need to "show the clubs" first. There would be time enough to show them after

West made the opening lead.

Declarer won West's ♡J opening lead with the ♡Q and let the ♣6 ride to East's ♣Q. Thinking there might be two ace-queen doubletons in this deal, East returned a heart.

Declarer won the ♡A and led his last club. East won, but declarer took his nine tricks: five clubs, three hearts and a spade.

How many tricks do you think South took in 3NT at the other table?

There North transferred to clubs before putting South in 3NT. South captured West's ♡J opening lead with the ♡A and led the ♣4 to Trick 2. West covered with the ♣5. East, Stella by Starlight, captured dummy's ♣7 with the ♣Q.

Just as the other three players were turning their cards to the trick, the ♠K fell out of Stella's hand. Now the best that declarer could do was three tricks in each major and one diamond. Down two.

"Lucky, lucky," said Stella. "If I'd been awake, you'd be down three."

"Yes, Stella," said Moshe, West. "If you'd doubled two spades for the lead, you'd have saved your king."

DEAL 114. MR. SMUG STOPS THE OVERTRICK

```
                    ♠ K Q J 8 6
                    ♡ 8 4
                    ◇ 6 5 2
                    ♣ K Q 7            Mr. Smug
   ♠ 7 5 2                             ♠ A 9 3
   ♡ Q 10 7 6                          ♡ 5 3
   ◇ 9 8 7                             ◇ A 10 4 3
   ♣ 6 5 2                             ♣ A J 8 3
                    ♠ 10 4
                    ♡ A K J 9 2
                    ◇ K Q J
                    ♣ 10 9 4
```

Despite East's takeout double of North's 1♠ response to 1♡, South and North crept up to 3NT. West led the ◇9 to East's ◇A. South dropped a crafty ◇Q.

South won East's ◇3 return with ◇K to start spades with the ♠10. West signaled count with the ♠2, so East knew to duck the first spade and win the next. A third diamond went to South's ◇J.

Declarer led the ♣3 to dummy's ♣Q, but East won the ♣A.

"No overtrick for you this time!" he said as he cashed the ◇10.

That was all for the defense, however. Soon declarer had his nine tricks: four spades, one club and two tricks in each red suit. Making 3NT.

When East and West compared scores with their teammates, they saw that in the other room South has marked his 3NT as *down* three.

"I know that you're very clever, Willie, but you must have mis-scored the board. Don't you mean *making* three? *Nobody* could go down three!" said Mr. Smug, his East teammate.

"No," said Willie. "It's that idiot Moshe. He fooled me with a play so stupid I didn't think even he could find it. I'll be writing it up for my new book on *Idiot Coups*.

"After a diamond to his ace, he shifted to—get this!—the club jack. I unblocked the ten, won in dummy, led to my ten of spades and back to dummy's jack. Moshe took his ace and returned a diamond. Desperate to reach dummy, I led the club four, finessed dummy's seven, and ... HELP!"

Willie took only two tricks in each red suit and one in each black suit.

DEAL 115. TAKING OUT AN ENTRY

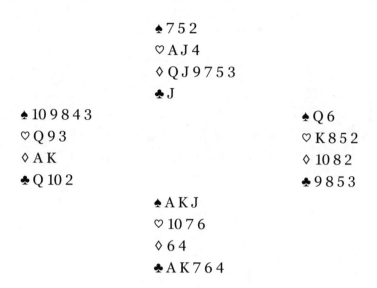

```
                    ♠ 7 5 2
                    ♡ A J 4
                    ◊ Q J 9 7 5 3
                    ♣ J
♠ 10 9 8 4 3                            ♠ Q 6
♡ Q 9 3                                 ♡ K 8 5 2
◊ A K                                   ◊ 10 8 2
♣ Q 10 2                                ♣ 9 8 5 3
                    ♠ A K J
                    ♡ 10 7 6
                    ◊ 6 4
                    ♣ A K 7 6 4
```

North gambled a 3NT raise of South's 1NT opening.

West led the ♠10 to East's ♠Q and declarer's ♠A. South led the ◊4 to West's ◊K. Hoping to catch East with ♠KQ6, West continued with the ♠8. Declarer won, led another diamond to West's ◊A and soon had ten tricks.

How did 3NT fail in the other room?

It took some doing. First South helped. He squelched West's hope of catching East with the ♠K by winning the ♠K at Trick 1.

Then East helped. When South led the ◊4 to Trick 2, East followed with the ◊2, a count card, so West could envision South's doubleton diamond and subsequent entry problem.

West counted East for at most 3 HCP. Where could those 3 HCP lie? Clubs? Even ♣K9xxx would not suffice. South could duck both a ♣Q shift and a ♣10 continuation. However, ♡K10xx would do, because a third heart lead would kill dummy's ♡A as an entry to the diamonds.

A low heart shift *requires* East to have the ♡10 with the ♡K, but the ♡Q needs only the ♡K. West led the ♡Q and declarer had no recourse.

Win now, or duck and wait for the third round to take dummy's ♡A? Either way, dummy's entry to the diamonds would be gone, and with it, all hope for nine tricks.

DEAL 116. KEEPING DECLARER FROM DUMMY

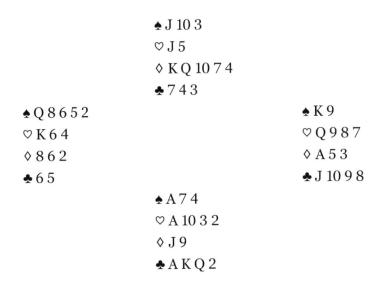

```
              ♠ J 10 3
              ♡ J 5
              ◇ K Q 10 7 4
              ♣ 7 4 3
♠ Q 8 6 5 2                      ♠ K 9
♡ K 6 4                          ♡ Q 9 8 7
◇ 8 6 2                          ◇ A 5 3
♣ 6 5                            ♣ J 10 9 8
              ♠ A 7 4
              ♡ A 10 3 2
              ◇ J 9
              ♣ A K Q 2
```

South opened 1♣, jump-shifted to 2♡ and settled in 3NT. West led a fourth-highest ♠5, East covered dummy's ♠J with the ♠K and declarer won the ♠A.

Declarer led the ◇J. When it won, he overtook the ◇9 with dummy's ◇10. East was watching the spots carefully for West's count signal. He won the second diamond and returned the ♠9 to West's ♠Q.

Now dummy's ♠10 remained as an entry to dummy's diamonds. Good discarding held declarer to 10 tricks: one heart, two spades, three clubs and four diamonds.

Could the defenders have stopped the overtrick?

What's that about stopping overtricks? Why not *beat the contract*?

It seemed natural to play the ♠K from ♠K9, under other circumstances a necessary unblocking play. But with dummy's diamonds looming, East needed above all to keep dummy's ♠10 from becoming an entry.

In the other room, defending 3NT on a slightly different auction, East withheld the ♠K at Trick 1. Three diamond tricks rotted in the now entryless dummy. Seven tricks instead of ten, and some discussion later between North and South whether to play the fancy Wolff Signoff convention.

DEAL 117. DECLARER TRIES TO FIND AN EXTRA ENTRY

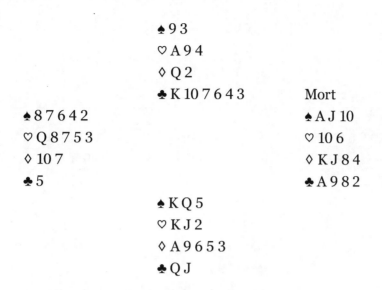

♠ 9 3
♡ A 9 4
◊ Q 2
♣ K 10 7 6 4 3

Mort

♠ 8 7 6 4 2
♡ Q 8 7 5 3
◊ 10 7
♣ 5

♠ A J 10
♡ 10 6
◊ K J 8 4
♣ A 9 8 2

♠ K Q 5
♡ K J 2
◊ A 9 6 5 3
♣ Q J

South opened 1NT as dealer and North raised to 3NT. West led a fourth-highest ♡6. East played a "third hand high" ♡10. South placed West with a finessable ♡Q and won with a deceptive ♡K.

East did well to duck the ♣Q and ♣J at Tricks 2 and 3.

Now declarer needed two dummy entries to bring dummy's clubs home. Thinking he could lead towards dummy's ◊Q later if necessary, he led the ♡2 now.

Placing East with the hidden ♡J, East followed with the ♡3 and South finessed dummy's ♡9 successfully. Dummy's ♣10 dislodged East's ♣A, and now declarer was playing for overtricks.

East, Post-Mortimer Snide, shook a critical finger at West afterwards and said, "Your fault, again, partner. Just fly with your queen when declarer leads the deuce of hearts at Trick 4, and down he goes."

"Oh yeah, Mort? If I do that you will have jack-ten doubleton and our opponents will start arguing which of them should have bid slam."

Who was right?

The defense in the other room provides an answer. East realized that he needed to keep the ♡10 to be able to beat dummy's ♡9 on the second round. So he covered West's ♡5 gently with the ♡6 at Trick 1. South placed East with ♡76 doubleton and won the ♡J, but no trickery could turn dummy's ♡9 into an entry now. 3NT went down.

DEAL 118. TIMING; TAKING AWAY ONE OF THE ENTRIES

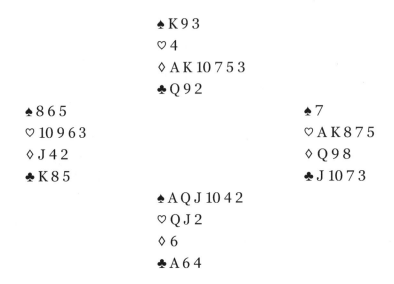

```
                      ♠ K 9 3
                      ♡ 4
                      ◇ A K 10 7 5 3
                      ♣ Q 9 2
    ♠ 8 6 5                            ♠ 7
    ♡ 10 9 6 3                         ♡ A K 8 7 5
    ◇ J 4 2                            ◇ Q 9 8
    ♣ K 8 5                            ♣ J 10 7 3
                      ♠ A Q J 10 4 2
                      ♡ Q J 2
                      ◇ 6
                      ♣ A 6 4
```

South opened 1♠ in second seat. North's game-forcing 2◇ response and subsequent 4♡ splinter rebid prompted South to cue-bid 5♣. Valuing ace-king-sixth greatly as a side suit, North bid a thin 6♠.

East won West's passive ♡10 opening lead with the ♡K and shifted to a "safe" ♣J. South rose with the ♣A and saw that he needed to establish dummy's diamonds to make. So he cashed dummy's ◇AK and ruffed a diamond high. Hallelujah, brother, they split 3-3. Declarer drew trump ending in dummy and dummy's three long diamonds provided enough discards for all his losers at the end. Making 6♠.

Do you see how the defenders beat 6♠ in the other room?

After winning the ♡K at Trick 1, East sacrificed the ♡A by leading it to Trick 2. That forced declarer to ruff in dummy. He could still ruff out the diamonds, but now he needed trumps to split 2-2. He needed to finish drawing them and end in dummy, as dummy no longer had a third trump to serve as a late entry to the good spades.

With no place to park his ♣Q, South went down one.

DEAL 119. CHOOSING WHEN DECLARER USES AN ENTRY

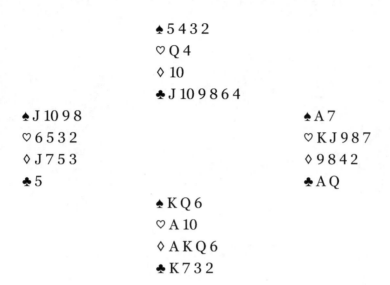

```
                      ♠ 5 4 3 2
                      ♡ Q 4
                      ◊ 10
                      ♣ J 10 9 8 6 4
        ♠ J 10 9 8                    ♠ A 7
        ♡ 6 5 3 2                     ♡ K J 9 8 7
        ◊ J 7 5 3                     ◊ 9 8 4 2
        ♣ 5                           ♣ A Q
                      ♠ K Q 6
                      ♡ A 10
                      ◊ A K Q 6
                      ♣ K 7 3 2
```

North raised South's 2NT opening to 3NT in hope that his long clubs would supply the necessary tricks.

East won West's ♠J opening lead with the ♠A, and returned the ♠7 woodenly. Perhaps he didn't realize that it was too much to expect more than another jack from West.

South won the ♠K. With no clue which honor was more likely to be singleton, he led the ♣K to Trick 3. East won the ♣A and shifted to the ◊9. Declarer won the ◊A, led a club to East's ♣Q, and soon had 10 tricks.

Was East, who had opening strength himself, helpless to beat 3NT?

In the other room, East won the ♠A at Trick 1 and thought to set up hearts, but any heart shift would blow a trick. Still, with two possible club stoppers, she might be able to afford a heart gambit. Alas, if she let dummy win a trick with the ♡Q now, one of her club stoppers would disappear.

Then it dawned on her. If declarer had to win the ♡A first, she could retain both club stoppers, as declarer could not lead clubs through her.

Accordingly, she led the heart king to Trick 2.

South was toast. He could not reach dummy to lead clubs through East without burning dummy's ♡Q, the only remaining heart stopper. So he led the ♣K trying to spear a singleton ♣Q. East won, led to dummy's ♡Q, and wound up with six tricks before declarer could get nine.

DEAL 120. DEFENDER DUCKS TO DESTROY A DUMMY ENTRY

```
                    ♠ K Q 8 4 2
                    ♡ Q 10 4
                    ◇ 10 8
                    ♣ 8 6 4
  ♠ 9 5                              ♠ A J 10 6
  ♡ 6 3 2                            ♡ 5
  ◇ K Q 9 4                          ◇ J 7 5 3 2
  ♣ K 9 5 3                          ♣ Q J 10
                    ♠ 7 3
                    ♡ A K J 9 8 7
                    ◇ A 6
                    ♣ A 7 2
```

West led the ◇K against South's 4♡. Declarer won the ◇A and led the ♠3. West played the ♠9 and East captured dummy's ♠Q with the ♠A. East cashed the ◇J and shifted to the ♣Q.

South won the ♣A, led to dummy's ♠K and ruffed a spade high. He cashed a heart honor and led low to dummy's ♡10.

Dummy's fifth spade let declarer discard a club and declarer had one trump left for his tenth trick.

Do you see how East could have beaten 4♡?

In the other room, East took advantage of West's ♠9 play, a count signal at Trick 2, and ducked the first spade.

This dummy entry did little good for declarer, and he could not use it to ruff a spade as South had done at the first table.

South was an entry short of the three he needed to ruff out the spades and cash dummy's fifth spade. He lost one spade, one diamond, and two clubs.
Down one.

DEAL 121. REMOVING DECLARER'S ENTRY

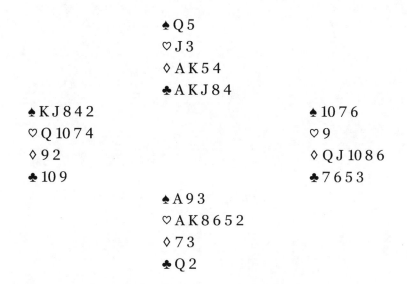

```
                        ♠ Q 5
                        ♡ J 3
                        ◊ A K 5 4
                        ♣ A K J 8 4
      ♠ K J 8 4 2                        ♠ 10 7 6
      ♡ Q 10 7 4                         ♡ 9
      ◊ 9 2                              ◊ Q J 10 8 6
      ♣ 10 9                             ♣ 7 6 5 3
                        ♠ A 9 3
                        ♡ A K 8 6 5 2
                        ◊ 7 3
                        ♣ Q 2
```

When North opened 1♣ and reversed into 2◊. South sniffed slam and jumped to 3♡. North's 4♡ encouraged him further, and he cue-bid 4♠. spurring North to bid 6♡.

West led the ♣10. Declarer won the ♣Q and to guard against the actual 4-1 heart split, he continued with the ♡2. West rose with the ♡Q and saw the futility of a club continuation. So he shifted to the ◊9, but that was the end of the defense.

Declarer won in dummy and unblocked dummy's ♡J. He entered his hand with the ♠A, finished trumps and ran clubs to discard his remaining spades. Making 6♡.

Well declared, but could the defenders have beaten 6♡?

The expert player and bridge writer Frank Stewart was West in the other room, and reported this deal in his syndicated newspaper column several years ago. After he won the ♡Q, he shifted to the ♠K to drive out South's only safe hand entry.

Declarer won the ♠A and unblocked dummy's ♡J, but Frank could overruff whichever minor South ruffed to return to his hand and finish trumps. No escape from down one.

Neat play, Frank. This game might be a bit too tough for us.

DEAL 122. REMOVING AN ENTRY FROM DUMMY

```
                    ♠ K Q J
                    ♡ K 10
                    ◊ A Q 7 6 5
                    ♣ 10 9 6
        ♠ 2                             ♠ A 10 9 8 5 3
        ♡ 9 7 3 2                       ♡ void
        ◊ 9 8 3                         ◊ K J 10 2
        ♣ A Q 7 4 2                     ♣ J 8 5
                    ♠ 7 6 4
                    ♡ A Q J 8 6 5 4
                    ◊ 4
                    ♣ K 3
```

South opened 4♡ on favorable vulnerability and North made a disciplined pass. West led the ♠2 to East's ♠A and ruffed East's ♠10 return. Reading the ♠10 correctly as showing preference for diamonds over clubs, West shifted to the ◊9.

Now South worked on ruffing out the diamonds. ◊A, diamond ruff, heart to dummy's ♡10, diamond ruff high, heart to dummy's ♡K and another diamond ruff high. South's remaining trump honor drew West's last trump.

A spade to dummy's ♠K let declarer discard a club on the ◊Q. South lost only one club and the two tricks lost initially.

4♡ made.

How did the defenders beat 4♡ in the other room?

In the other room, the defense against 4♡ began the same way. However, after ruffing the spade, West recognized East's ♠10 as suit preference showing the ◊K, but not as a command to lead diamonds.

Fearing that South might ruff out dummy's diamonds, West led the ♡3, removing a vital entry from dummy. This thoughtful play kept declarer from establishing the fifth diamond.

Down one.

DEAL 123. REMOVING A DUMMY ENTRY EARLY

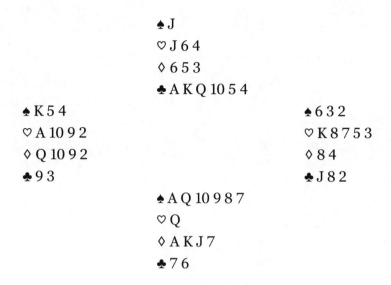

```
              ♠ J
              ♡ J 6 4
              ◊ 6 5 3
              ♣ A K Q 10 5 4
♠ K 5 4                        ♠ 6 3 2
♡ A 10 9 2                     ♡ K 8 7 5 3
◊ Q 10 9 2                     ◊ 8 4
♣ 9 3                          ♣ J 8 2
              ♠ A Q 10 9 8 7
              ♡ Q
              ◊ A K J 7
              ♣ 7 6
```

South wangled tertiary spade support from North to reach 4♠.

West led the ♡A, the unbid suit, and catching an encouraging ♡8 from East, continued the ♡10 after South's ♡Q fell.

South ruffed and played ♠A then ♠Q to drive out West's ♠K. West persisted with the ♡9. South ruffed East's ♡K, drew the remaining trumps and ran clubs. Making 4♠ with an overtrick.

West's "forcing" defense was futile. What might have been effective?

In the other room, West stared at the dummy after his ♡A opening lead felled declarer's ♡Q. He saw those oh too solid clubs and decided to kill them by leading them while he still had trump control.

Soon West regained the lead with his ♠K on the second round of trumps. He persisted with his last club.

With the lead in dummy for the last time, South tried a diamond finesse, but West captured the ◊J with his ◊Q. He exited with the ♡10, and scored a fourth-round diamond trick at Trick 13.

Down one.

DEAL 124. SECOND SUIT DEFENSE

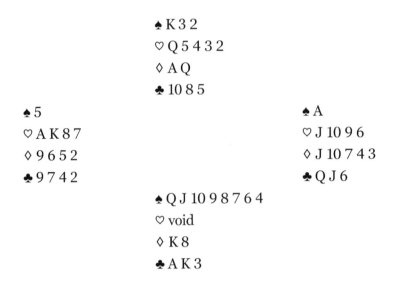

♠ K 3 2
♥ Q 5 4 3 2
♦ A Q
♣ 10 8 5

♠ 5
♥ A K 8 7
♦ 9 6 5 2
♣ 9 7 4 2

♠ A
♥ J 10 9 6
♦ J 10 7 4 3
♣ Q J 6

♠ Q J 10 9 8 7 6 4
♥ void
♦ K 8
♣ A K 3

North's 2♡ response to 1♠ was forcing only one round but promised a rebid unless opener raised. That allowed South to bide his time with a gentle 2♠ rebid. When North raised to 3♠, South cue-bid 4♣. North cooperated with a 4♢ cue bid in return. That sufficed for South to bid 6♠.

West led the ♡A. Most who normally lead "ace from ace-king" revert to old-fashioned king-leads against slams. Leading the ♡A might induce declarer to try a ruffing finesse against East's imagined ♡K later.

Declarer ruffed and led the ♠J to East's ♠A. East exited passively in hearts. Declarer ruffed again and entered dummy twice in diamonds to ruff two more hearts. Dummy's ♠K provided the late entry he needed to discard a club on the established ♡Q. 6♠ made.

This is not the first time we've looked at deals where dummy has a long side suit. What's the best plan for defenders on such deals?

In the other room, East saw the danger posed by dummy's five-card suit. Instead of helping declarer ruff out the hearts, he shifted to diamonds when he got in with his ♠A, *killing a dummy entry* that declarer could otherwise use effectively later.

In the end, declarer had to lose a club. Down one.

DEAL 125. THIRD HAND LOW TO KILL DUMMY'S ENTRY

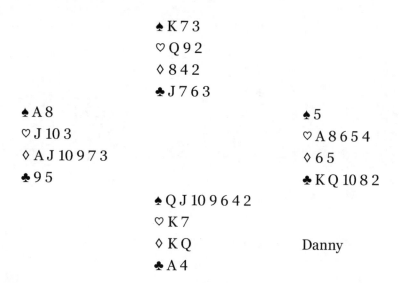

```
                    ♠ K 7 3
                    ♡ Q 9 2
                    ◊ 8 4 2
                    ♣ J 7 6 3
    ♠ A 8                             ♠ 5
    ♡ J 10 3                          ♡ A 8 6 5 4
    ◊ A J 10 9 7 3                    ◊ 6 5
    ♣ 9 5                             ♣ K Q 10 8 2
                    ♠ Q J 10 9 6 4 2
                    ♡ K 7
                    ◊ K Q             Danny
                    ♣ A 4
```

Who's saving against whom? Until bridge theorists can appraise North's ♡9 here, we won't always know.

After West overcalled 2◊, North raised to 2♠ and East showed Sergeant Pepper's favorite suits with a misleadingly named "responsive" double, South didn't worry about that. He just shot out 4♠.

West led the ♡J. Declarer played low from dummy. East turned to Southeast and said, "I know what you say about not playing aces on air, Danny, but this time I think it's right."

South said, "Whose king are you calling air?" and dropped the ♡K.

East led the ♣K, which drove out South's ♣A. Then South finessed dummy's ♡9, discarded the ♣4 on dummy's ♡Q, and started trumps. Their three aces were the only tricks the defenders took. 4♠ made.

In the post-mortem with her teammates, who had failed in 4♠, West asked, "Didn't you unblock the heart king? You'd better reread Dr J's book on Unblocking."

"No," the unsuccessful declarer replied. "I won the heart king. You must have misdefended."

Huh? In the other room, East let the ♡J ride to South's ♡K. A heart to dummy's ♡9 drove out East's ♡A, but now East's ♣K shift established his ♣Q as the setting trick before declarer could reach dummy to cash the ♡Q.

DEAL 126. THIRD HAND LOW TO BLOCK THE ENTRY

```
                        ♠ Q J 10
                        ♡ 7 2
                        ◇ 8 3
                        ♣ A Q J 9 8 4
    ♠ 9 7 6 4 2                             ♠ K 5 3
    ♡ Q 6 3                                 ♡ J 10 8 5
    ◇ Q 7 5                                 ◇ A 6 4
    ♣ 7 3                                   ♣ K 5 2
                        ♠ A 8
                        ♡ A K 9 4
                        ◇ K J 10 9 2
                        ♣ 10 6
```

Hands with a four-card red suit, a five-card minor and two doubletons are best treated as balanced for notrump-bidding purposes, so South opened 1NT and North raised to 3NT.

West led the ♠7, second highest from length and weakness. East covered dummy's ♠10 with the ♠K. Declarer won the ♠A, and worked on clubs, letting the ♣10 ride.

East ducked, but captured dummy's ♣J when declarer continued clubs. East shifted to hearts, but declarer won, crossed to dummy in spades and wound up with ten tricks.

Was there any chance for the defense?

Not after Trick 1. In the other room, East ducked the first spade, the right play even if West's spot-card lead had been fourth highest. Declarer came to his hand with the ♡A and worked on clubs, but East ducked the first and won the second.

The rest of dummy's clubs went to waste, as dummy was bereft of entries.

Eventually declarer came to seven tricks. Down two.

DEAL 127. THIRD HAND SAVES A
HIGH CARD TO KILL ENTRY

```
                    ♠ J 9 6
                    ♡ J 6
                    ◇ 7 6
                    ♣ Q J 10 7 6 5
      ♠ K 10 8 2                      ♠ Q 7 4
      ♡ 9 4 3                         ♡ K 10 8 2
      ◇ Q 9 8 2                       ◇ J 10 3
      ♣ 9 8                           ♣ A 3 2
                    ♠ A 5 3
                    ♡ A Q 7 5
                    ◇ A K 5 4
                    ♣ K 4
```

Hoping that the long clubs could provide enough tricks, North raised South's 2NT opening to 3NT.

With a close choice between diamond and spade opening leads, West was guided by North's failure to use a Jacoby Transfer or Stayman to lead the ♠2.

Declarer inserted dummy's ♠9 and captured East's ♠Q with the ♠A to start clubs. East ducked South's ♣K but won the next club with his ♣A,

South won East's ◇A shift with the ◇A and led a spade towards dummy. Soon declarer cashed out for ten tricks.

How did the defense prevail in the other room?

There West also led the ♠2 against 3NT. Noticing that the ♠J was a likely outside entry to dummy's clubs if she released the ♠Q now, East ducked.

With dummy's potential outside entry disabled, declarer could take only seven tricks instead of 10 or 11.

CREATING, FINDING, UNBLOCKING & DISCARDING

DEAL 128. CAN "WRONG-SIDING" BE RIGHT?

```
                        ♠ A K 8
                        ♡ K 2
                        ◊ Q J 10 9 5 3
                        ♣ A 6              Willie
        ♠ 10 9 5 3 2                       ♠ J 7
        ♡ 8 3                              ♡ A Q J 7 4
        ◊ K 7                              ◊ 6 2
        ♣ 8 5 4 2 Jim                      ♣ Q J 10 7
                        ♠ Q 6 4
                        ♡ 10 9 6 5
                        ◊ A 8 4
                        ♣ K 9 3
```

Jim faced a problem when North opened 1◊ and East overcalled 1♡ with both sides vul. His hand looked right for 1NT, but was ten-nine-fourth really a heart stopper? Jim bid 1NT anyway and North raised to 3NT.

West led the ♡8. Jim covered with dummy's ♡K. East won the ♡A and said, "Looks like you wrong-sided the notrumps again, Jim. Who do you think you are, the Hideous Hog?"

Jim grinned and said, "He who laughs last laughs best, Willie."

Willie cashed two more hearts and exited with a fourth heart. Jim won, crossed to dummy in spades and took a diamond finesse into the safe hand. It lost, but West could not reach Willie to let him cash his long heart.

Jim scored up +600 but politely refrained from laughing.

What do you think happened to Danny, South in the other room?

"I right-sided the notrumps," said Danny later. "Ursula might have opened one notrump, as we can do with18 points, but chose one diamond. One notrump would not be wrong, but I bid two diamonds, hoping Ursula could bid notrumps. She did, and I raised to three.

"East led the seven of hearts instead of the queen. Ursula won the king, but when the diamond finesse lost, the poor soul went down one."

"Hmmm," said Jim. "Willie could have beaten me the same way, by playing the seven of hearts at Trick One to retain the link between hands."

```
                        ♠ 10 8 3
                        ♡ A 9 7 6 4
                        ◊ K 9
                        ♣ 6 5 2
        ♠ K J 9 7 6                        ♠ A Q 2
        ♡ 8 2                              ♡ Q 5
        ◊ J 4 2                            ◊ 8 7 6 5
        ♣ A Q 4                            ♣ 10 9 8 3
                        ♠ 5 4
                        ♡ K J 10 3
                        ◊ A Q 10 3
                        ♣ K J 7
```

South opened 1◊. West overcalled 1♠, and North's "Negative Double" (showing hearts) enabled South to bid 3♡ after East raised to 2♠.

West led the ♠7, East played a "third hand high" ♠A and shifted to the ♣10. Good shift, through declarer's likely strength and up to partner's!

Ready to nominate East as "Defensive Player of the Year"?

Declarer covered gently with the ♣J, West won the ♣Q ... and?

Oops, problem! Did South have the hand shown above or did he have seemingly equally plausible (b) ♠Q4 ♡KJ103 ◊AQ103 ♣J87?

West voted for Hand (b) and cashed the ♠K and ♣A. When the ♡Q popped up doubleton on the second round, South claimed. Making 3♡.

The defenders could have taken five fast tricks in the black suits. Apportion the blame for not taking them.

All blame to East! East could read West for the ♠K at the start, not only from the auction but from the Rule of 11, which revealed that South had no spade higher that the ♠7. So, win Trick 1 with the ♠Q, shift to the ♣10, win Trick 3 with the ♠A and lead the ♣9. Five easy tricks.

When East didn't play the ♠Q, West could infer that South had it. In the other room, East won the ♠Q at Trick 1. Her ♣10 shift beat 3♡.

DEAL 130. WHOSE ENTRY TO SAVE:
YOUR OWN OR PARTNER'S?

```
                         ♠ A J 5
                         ♡ 10 6
                         ◇ J 10 9 7 6
                         ♣ Q J 4
         ♠ 9 8 7 4 2                        ♠ K 10
         ♡ 5 4 3                            ♡ A K 9 8 2
         ◇ K 4                              ◇ 3 2
         ♣ 8 6 5                            ♣ 10 9 7 3
                         ♠ Q 6 3
                         ♡ Q J 7
                         ◇ A Q 8 5
                         ♣ A K 2
```

East opened a slightly shaded 1♡ in third seat. South overcalled a "15 to 18" HCP 1NT and carried on to 3NT when North raised to 2NT,

Playing "low from any three," opening leads, West led the ♡3, covered promptly by dummy's ♡10. Viewing his ♠K as a sure entry, East played the ♡A, ♡K and ♡9 in that order, emphasizing his preference for spades.

Upon winning Trick 3, declarer crossed to dummy's ♣J to start diamonds with dummy's ◇J. West won the ◇K and shifted to the ♠9, but declarer rose with dummy's ♠A and had nine tricks: four diamonds, three clubs, and one in each major. East is still waiting with his ♠K and ♡83.

Could the defenders have beaten 3NT?

In the other room, they did. After the same auction, West led a "top of nothing" ♡5. East, Moshe, saw those five threatening diamonds in dummy, and appreciated that South might not need more than one trick in spades.

Beating 3NT looked hopeless unless West could stop diamonds and had three hearts. So Moshe let dummy's ♡10 hold Trick 1. Declarer was in dummy to finesse diamonds immediately.

West won the ◇K and continued with the ♡4 to beat the contract.

DEAL 131. CREATING AN ENTRY FOR PARTNER

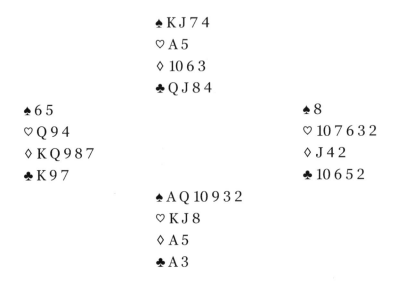

                         ♠ K J 7 4
                         ♡ A 5
                         ♢ 10 6 3
                         ♣ Q J 8 4

♠ 6 5   ♠ 8
♡ Q 9 4   ♡ 10 7 6 3 2
♢ K Q 9 8 7   ♢ J 4 2
♣ K 9 7   ♣ 10 6 5 2

                         ♠ A Q 10 9 3 2
                         ♡ K J 8
                         ♢ A 5
                         ♣ A 3

After West overcalled 2♢ on favorable vulnerability and North made a 3♠ "limit raise," South cue-bid 4♢ to try for slam. When North cooperated with a 4♡ cue bid in return, South bid 6♠ without further ado.

West led the ♢K. South won the ♢A, drew trump and stripped the hearts by ruffing the ♡J in dummy. Then he ran all but one of his trumps to reach a four-card ending:

                                 North: ♠none   ♡none   ♢106   ♣QJ

West: ♠none   ♡none   ♢Q9   ♣K9

                                 South: ♠2   ♡none   ♢5   ♣A3

When South led the ♠2, what could West do? If he discarded the ♣9, then his ♣K would fall. If he discarded the ♢9, declarer could throw him in with his ♢Q and force him to lead from ♣K9 at Trick 12. He chose to discard the ♢9, hoping that declarer would think he had blanked the ♣K earlier.

Declarer exited in diamonds and West had to lead clubs for him. Making 6♠.

In the other room, North and South reached 6♠ on a different auction. How did the defenders beat 6♠ there?

Very simply. Not wanting to be thrown in with the ♢Q at Trick 12, he discarded her at Trick 10, hoping East held the ♢J, his only chance. East obliged, winning Trick 11 with the ♢J to lead a club through. Down one!

DEAL 132. CREATING AN ENTRY FOR PARTNER

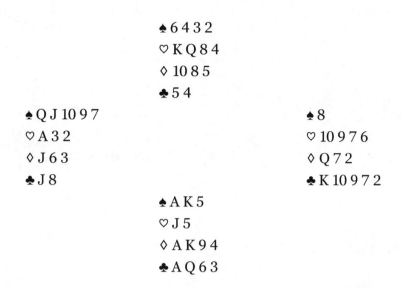

  ♠ 6 4 3 2
  ♡ K Q 8 4
  ◊ 10 8 5
  ♣ 5 4

♠ Q J 10 9 7   ♠ 8
♡ A 3 2   ♡ 10 9 7 6
◊ J 6 3   ◊ Q 7 2
♣ J 8   ♣ K 10 9 7 2

  ♠ A K 5
  ♡ J 5
  ◊ A K 9 4
  ♣ A Q 6 3

South opened 2NT and reached 3NT via Stayman. West led the ♠Q. South won the ♠K. He cashed the ◊A and ◊K early, catching low diamonds from both defenders. Then he led the ♡J. West won the ♡A and continued with the ♠9. East discarded the ♣2 and declarer won the ♠A.

Declarer cashed dummy's ♡K and ♡Q, discarding the ♣3. Then he finessed the ♣Q successfully and led the ◊4. East won and cashed the ♡10, but declarer had his nine tricks: three diamonds, and two tricks in every other suit.

How did the defenders beat 3NT in the other room?

East appreciated the need for West to obtain the lead to set up and cash the setting tricks in spades. Seeing declarer play diamonds from the top, she placed West with a likely entry in the form of the ◊J. Therefore she dumped her ◊Q on the second diamond, keeping the ◊6 to lead to West.

West was equally alert. Realizing that dummy had no entries except in hearts, he ducked declarer's ♡J and watched carefully for East's count signal. East cooperated with the ♡10 and West knew to take his ♡A on the second round.

When South played a third diamond to set up a fourth, West won the ◊J and cashed the good spades. Three spades, one diamond and one heart sank 3NT.

DEAL 133. THE MORPHY COUP

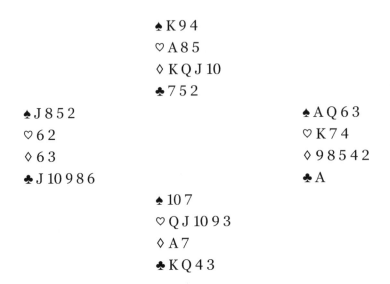

```
                    ♠ K 9 4
                    ♡ A 8 5
                    ♦ K Q J 10
                    ♣ 7 5 2
  ♠ J 8 5 2                          ♠ A Q 6 3
  ♡ 6 2                              ♡ K 7 4
  ♦ 6 3                              ♦ 9 8 5 4 2
  ♣ J 10 9 8 6                       ♣ A
                    ♠ 10 7
                    ♡ Q J 10 9 3
                    ♦ A 7
                    ♣ K Q 4 3
```

North responded a game-forcing 2♦ to South's 1♡ opening, and raised South's 2♡ rebid to 3♡. South had nothing to bid but 4♡.

West led the ♣J to East's ♣A. On the auction, West could have nothing more than another jack. East could just "see" declarer's two spade losers about to disappear on dummy's diamonds. Despairingly, he cashed his ♠A while it was still cashable.

The ♡K was the only other trick for the defense. 4♡ made.

Given West's failure to find a killing spade opening lead (we wouldn't find it either), do you see how a truly desperate East could have obtained the club ruff that would beat 4♡?

In the other room, West also "failed" to find the killing spade lead against 4♡, but East was a former women's chess champion. She had a habit of asking herself, "What would Paul Morphy do?"

Answer: *visualize the checkmate* and *sacrifice the queen*. In this position, the piece she saw administering the decisive check was the ♠J ... in West's hand. To turn him into an entry she led the ♠Q.

A pleasantly surprised declarer won dummy's ♠K and played three rounds of diamonds to discard the ♠10. West ruffed and returned a club for East to ruff. Then East waited to win the ♡K. Down one the hard way.

DEAL 134. TRUMP PROMOTION OR SHOW YOUR ENTRY

```
                    ♠ 9 6
                    ♡ Q 5 2
                    ◇ 8 4 3
                    ♣ A Q 10 8 3
     ♠ 5 4 2                        ♠ 8 7
     ♡ 4                            ♡ A K J 10 8 7 3
     ◇ 9 7 6 5 2                    ◇ A
     ♣ 9 7 6 4                      ♣ J 5 2
                    ♠ A K Q J 10 3
                    ♡ 9 6
                    ◇ K Q J 10
                    ♣ K
```

With nobody vul, East opened 4♡ in third seat, knowing there was little hope of slam but much hope of shutting out spades. As usual, spades won the battle of the majors; South's 4♠ bought the contract.

West led the ♡4. East won the ♡10 and continued with the ♡A, suit preference for diamonds. Then he led the ♡K, hoping West had as little as a doubleton queen or tripleton jack of spades to overruff declarer.

No such luck. Declarer ruffed ostentatiously with the ♠A, drew trumps, dislodged the ◇A and claimed his 4♠ contract.

Could East have done better?

In the other room, East saw a sure way to beat 4♠. As the ♡4 was the lowest missing heart, it was surely a singleton.

So after winning the ♡10 at Trick 1, East cashed the ◇A and led the ♡J, unmistakable suit preference for diamonds.

West ruffed and gave East a diamond ruff. Down one.

DEAL 135. TRY TO CREATE YOUR OWN ENTRY

```
                        ♠ Q 8 4 2
                        ♡ 4 3 2
                        ◇ 4 2
          Moshe         ♣ K J 6 5         Millie
          ♠ 9 3                           ♠ 6 5
          ♡ A 7 6                         ♡ Q J 10 9
          ◇ Q J 9 7                       ◇ K 10 6 3
          ♣ A 10 9 4                      ♣ 8 7 2
                        ♠ A K J 10 7
                        ♡ K 8 5
                        ◇ A 8 5
                        ♣ Q 3
```

South did well to open 1♠, for in his partnership's methods he could rebid 2NT over partner's response to show the same strength as a 1NT opening. Had his five-card suit been any other, he would have had to open 1NT lest a one-over-one response handcuff him. North raised to 2♠, and signed off with 3♠ over South's 2NT game try.

West led the ◇Q. East encouraged with the ◇10 and South let the ◇Q hold. South won the second diamond with the ◇A, cashed the ♠A, and overtook his ♠J with dummy's ♠Q when West's ♠9 appeared.

Then he led low to his ♣Q. West won the ♣A and returned the ♣4 to dummy's ♣J. South dumped a heart on dummy's ♣K and led low to his ♡K. West won the ♡A and returned a heart to East. That was the fourth trick for the defense and the last. Declarer lost two hearts and one trick in each minor to make 3♠.

East, Thoroughly Modern Millie, was not pleased. She said, "If only you'd agreed to play Upside-Down Signals, we could have untangled things and gotten our three heart tricks."

Was Thoroughly Modern Millie right?

No, she was thoroughly wrong. In the other room, East knew he needed to get in to lead the ♡Q through. He overtook West's ◇Q with the ◇K, implying the ◇10. South won the ◇A, drew trump, and drove out West's ♣A. Trusting East to have the ◇10, West led the ◇7. East won the ◇10 and led the ♡Q. Three heart tricks put 3♠ down one.

DEAL 136. DISCARDING TO CREATE ENTRIES

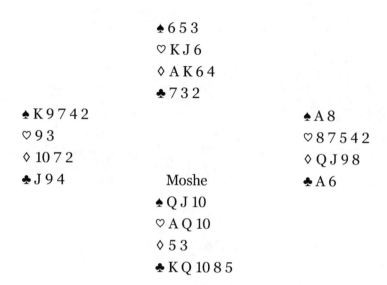

```
              ♠ 6 5 3
              ♡ K J 6
              ◇ A K 6 4
              ♣ 7 3 2
♠ K 9 7 4 2                      ♠ A 8
♡ 9 3                           ♡ 8 7 5 4 2
◇ 10 7 2                        ◇ Q J 9 8
♣ J 9 4           Moshe         ♣ A 6
              ♠ Q J 10
              ♡ A Q 10
              ◇ 5 3
              ♣ K Q 10 8 5
```

Players who don't appreciate the value of tens that accompany other honors in their suits would open 1♣ and reach game in three rounds, but Moshe opened a good-15-to-18 HCP 1NT. North raised directly to 3NT.

West led the ♠4 to East's ♠A. South dropped the ♠J and covered East's ♠8 return with the ♠Q; just keeping in practice to try to confuse things. West won the ♠K and continued with the ♠2. Who knows whether he intended it to show a fifth spade, or to show suit preference for clubs?

"One good deuce deserves another," said East as he threw the ♡2.

South won the ♠10, crossed to dummy in hearts and led a club through East. South won the ♣K and crossed to dummy in diamonds to lead another club. East won the ♣A perforce. South claimed an overtrick.

How could the defenders have beaten 3NT?

In the other room, South reached game via 1♣-1◇; 1NT-2NT; 3NT. After the same spade lead, return and continuation, East realized that the only hope of an entry to West's spades lay in clubs. As little as jack-third could be a stopper and an entry, provided that ... East discarded the blocking ♣A on the third round of spades.

This East did. With only two club tricks coming, South's 10 tricks had turned to eight. Down one!

143

DEAL 137. DISCARDING TO CREATE ENTRIES

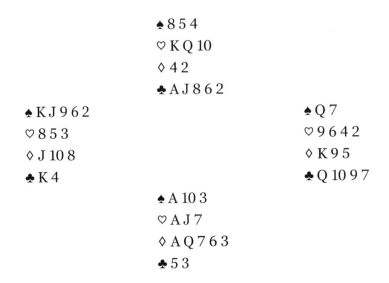

                   ♠ 8 5 4
                   ♡ K Q 10
                   ◊ 4 2
                   ♣ A J 8 6 2

♠ K J 9 6 2   ♠ Q 7
♡ 8 5 3   ♡ 9 6 4 2
◊ J 10 8   ◊ K 9 5
♣ K 4   ♣ Q 10 9 7

                   ♠ A 10 3
                   ♡ A J 7
                   ◊ A Q 7 6 3
                   ♣ 5 3

Another boring 1NT-3NT auction, and another fourth-highest spade lead. Declarer let East hold the ♠Q and ducked East's spade return. West continued the ♠2 and East joked, "When you can't follow suit, follow rank," as he discarded the ♡2.

Declarer won and saw that his best bet was to catch a 3-3 diamond break with the ◊K on side. So, heart to dummy, diamond, intending to let East win if he played the ◊K or finesse the ◊Q if East played some other diamond. When the finesse worked, declarer led another heart to dummy and then dummy's last diamond.

East played low again, so declarer won the ◊A, and led a low diamond. East was forced to overtake West's ◊J, and soon declarer was home free with four diamonds, three hearts, and two black aces. Making 3NT with a sigh of relief.

Both East and South erred. Do you see how?

In the other room, play was the same for the first two tricks. But on the third spade, East discarded the ◊K. Now declarer could not set up the diamonds without putting West in to cash the setting tricks in spades.

South erred in both rooms. By winning the second spade instead of waiting to win the third, South could have deprived East of the chance to make a good unblocking discard.

DEAL 138. ANOTHER ENTRY FOR PARTNER

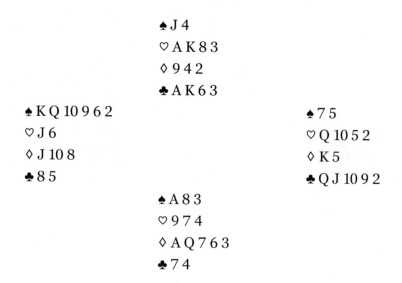

```
              ♠ J 4
              ♡ A K 8 3
              ◊ 9 4 2
              ♣ A K 6 3
♠ K Q 10 9 6 2                    ♠ 7 5
♡ J 6                             ♡ Q 10 5 2
◊ J 10 8                          ◊ K 5
♣ 8 5                             ♣ Q J 10 9 2
              ♠ A 8 3
              ♡ 9 7 4
              ◊ A Q 7 6 3
              ♣ 7 4
```

At favorable vulnerability, West opened a Weak 2♠ Bid. North doubled for takeout and South bid a natural constructive 2NT. North gambled a 3NT raise, you know, "vulnerable at IMPs" and all that jazz.

Yes, the "IMP odds" justify bidding games that have somewhat less than 40% chances when vulnerable at IMPs, but who can calculate such chances?

West led the ♠Q, hoping East could unblock the ♠J if he had it and avoiding a "Bath Coup" if declarer ducked with ♠AJx. South had only ♠A83 but ducked anyway and ducked West's ♠K next.

After winning the third spade, declarer crossed to dummy's ♡K to start diamonds. When East rose with the ◊K, South let it hold. After winning East's heart return in dummy, South took the next four diamonds and two top clubs. A total of nine tricks, making 3NT.

What do you think of the declarer play and the defense?

Not so hot. In the other room, South reached 3NT by a different route. He too ducked the first two spades, but East unloaded the ◊K on the third. Down two when West got in with a diamond trick to run spades.

South would have done better to win the second spade, gambling on West having a sixth spade for his non-vul Weak Two. That would deprive East of the opportunity to make a spectacular unblocking play.

But can we be sure? Maybe South knew West often opened five-card Weak Twos on favorable vulnerability and East often discarded woodenly.

DEAL 139. DISCARDING TO CREATE ENTRIES

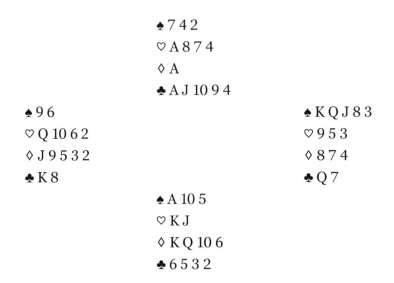

♠ 7 4 2
♥ A 8 7 4
♦ A
♣ A J 10 9 4

♠ 9 6
♥ Q 10 6 2
♦ J 9 5 3 2
♣ K 8

♠ K Q J 8 3
♥ 9 5 3
♦ 8 7 4
♣ Q 7

♠ A 10 5
♥ K J
♦ K Q 10 6
♣ 6 5 3 2

North opened 1♣ on favorable vulnerability and rebid 1♥. South bid 3NT without messing with an artificial fourth-suit rebid.

Taking note of the auction, West led the ♠9. Declarer ducked the first two spades and won the third as West discarded the ♦2, keeping "a guard at every door."

When declarer started clubs, West rose with the ♣K to unblock. Needing to keep East off lead, declarer let West's ♣K hold. West exited with the ♣8. Declarer guessed to play dummy's ♣A, felling East's ♣Q and romping home with ten tricks.

"Restricted choice," he said as he chalked up 430 points.

Could the defenders have beaten 3NT?

Yes. In the other room, West unloaded the blocking ♣K (which was doomed anyway if South had the ♣Q) on the third spade.

However, South erred also by giving East that chance. South could afford to lose one club and three spades, but not four spades. Thus he should win the second spade to keep West from discarding on the third.

South was also mistaken in thinking West had a "restricted choice." West would have no reason ever to play the ♣Q from king-queen-low, for South would never let the ♣Q hold. West had to play the ♣K whenever he had it, the sooner the better.

DEAL 140. FINDING PARTNER'S ENTRY BY INFERENCE

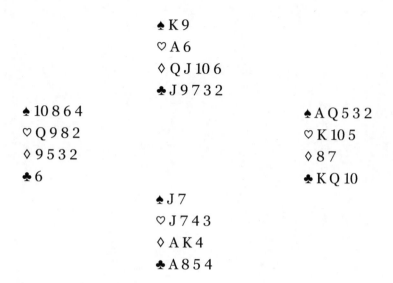

```
                        ♠ K 9
                        ♡ A 6
                        ◇ Q J 10 6
                        ♣ J 9 7 3 2
        ♠ 10 8 6 4                        ♠ A Q 5 3 2
        ♡ Q 9 8 2                         ♡ K 10 5
        ◇ 9 5 3 2                         ◇ 8 7
        ♣ 6                               ♣ K Q 10
                        ♠ J 7
                        ♡ J 7 4 3
                        ◇ A K 4
                        ♣ A 8 5 4
```

South opened 1♣ as dealer and passed North's limit jump raise.

West led the ♡2. Declarer won dummy's ♡A and started clubs with the ♣A and another.

East took his two club tricks, cashed his ♡K. shifted to the ◇8, and waited patiently for his two spade tricks.

He is still waiting for one of them, as declarer discarded the ♠7 on dummy's fourth diamond. 3♣ made, as declarer lost only two club tricks and one trick in each major.

On the same auction and opening lead, South failed to make 3♣ in the other room. Why so?

In the other room, East also placed West with very little strength. However, he knew West had the ♡Q. Else South, not knowing where the ♡K was, would surely let the lead come round to the ♡Q if he had it.

Therefore instead of cashing the ♡K after taking his trump tricks, East underled it to West's *known* ♡Q. West got the message and shifted to the ♠4. Down one.

Of course a sensible South would duck the opening lead, if only to sever the link between the defenders' hands.

DEAL 141. BY INFERENCE FROM THE OTHER SIDE

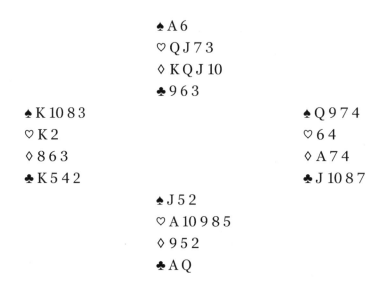

```
                        ♠ A 6
                        ♡ Q J 7 3
                        ◊ K Q J 10
                        ♣ 9 6 3
        ♠ K 10 8 3                      ♠ Q 9 7 4
        ♡ K 2                           ♡ 6 4
        ◊ 8 6 3                         ◊ A 7 4
        ♣ K 5 4 2                       ♣ J 10 8 7
                        ♠ J 5 2
                        ♡ A 10 9 8 5
                        ◊ 9 5 2
                        ♣ A Q
```

South responded 1♡ to North's 1◊ opening, and gambled 4♡ over North's 2♡ raise.

With a choice of black-suit leads, West let his stronger spade spot-cards sway him and led the ♠3.

Declarer won dummy's ♠A to start trumps promptly with dummy's ♡Q, which rode to West's ♡K. Fearing discards on dummy's diamonds, West cashed the ♠K and exited safely with the ♡2.

Declarer drove out East's ◊A. East's club shift came too late, and the diamond discard that West feared came soon enough. Away went South's ♣Q on North's fourth diamond, and 4♡ made.

What should West have thought and done after winning the ♡K?

West needed a club lead from East before, not after, the ◊A was dislodged. Could East have an entry other than the ◊A?

Yes. East might have the ♣A instead of the ◊A. However, almost surely East had the ♠Q. If *declarer* had the ♠Q, wouldn't he have let West's opening spade lead come round to her?

Did we say "almost surely"? Pardon us. The right word is *certainly*. Else East would not have signaled encouragingly with the ♠9 at Trick 1. In the other room, West paid attention to East's card. He underled to East's ♠Q. East's ♣J shift ensured down one.

DEAL 142. SECOND CHANCE

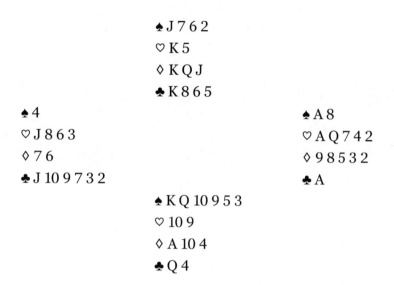

```
                    ♠ J 7 6 2
                    ♡ K 5
                    ◊ K Q J
                    ♣ K 8 6 5
    ♠ 4                            ♠ A 8
    ♡ J 8 6 3                      ♡ A Q 7 4 2
    ◊ 7 6                          ◊ 9 8 5 3 2
    ♣ J 10 9 7 3 2                 ♣ A
                    ♠ K Q 10 9 5 3
                    ♡ 10 9
                    ◊ A 10 4
                    ♣ Q 4
```

North and South used Jacoby Forcing Raises, the most popular of the many conventions that have replaced the natural forcing jump raises of an earlier era. North's 2NT response to 1♠ showed a *balanced* forcing raise and required opener to bid three in a void or singleton suit if he had one. Else he was required to show strength upside down with 3♠ (strongest), 3NT (moderate) or 4♠ (trashy) rebid.

Having only borderline opening strength, South jumped to 4♠.

West led the ♣J to East's ♣A. East had been asleep at the wheel during the auction. Now he regretted not overcalling 3♡ for the heart lead that would have scuttled 4♠, as South had advertised "No void or singleton!" East exited in diamonds and waited for Godot. Godot never came. 4♠ made.

Having not received a heart lead, did East get a *second chance?*

In the other room, South, vul against not, opened a Weak 2♠ Bid. North raised to 4♠. West led the same obvious but unfortunate ♣J. After East won the ♣A. he saw two chances. One was to catch West with the ◊A, unlikely given the vulnerability. The other was to catch West with three or four hearts headed by the ♡J.

To cater to both, East tried a Morphy Coup, shifting to the ♡Q to turn West's hoped-for ♡J into an entry. When West encouraged with the ♡8, East's plan succeeded: down one. Had West discouraged, East could shift to diamonds in time. A thoughtful defense that would work either way!

DEAL 143. CREATING AN ENTRY FOR PARTNER

```
                        ♠ J 10 6 5
                        ♡ K Q 5
                        ◇ 8 7 6 4
        Lilyan          ♣ 7 5
        ♠ 9 2                           ♠ A 3
        ♡ J 8 3                         ♡ A 10 9 7
        ◇ J 9 3                         ◇ Q 10 5 2
        ♣ A 10 8 6 2                    ♣ 9 4 3
                        ♠ K Q 8 7 4
                        ♡ 6 4 2
                        ◇ A K
                        ♣ K Q J
```

After South carried North's 2♠ raise of his 1♠ opening to 4♠, West had an ugly choice of opening leads and led a passive ♠2.

East won the ♠A and thought to lead through declarer's strength up to partner's. The mental coin that East flipped to choose between minors came up diamonds.

Declarer won East's ◇2 shift with the ◇A and drew one more round of trumps. He drove out West's ♣A to set up a discard for dummy's low heart. He held his losers to one each in every suit but diamonds. Making 4♠.

"Diamonds are for wearing, not leading," said Lilyan, West.

What did she mean by that?

We don't know, but in the other room, West led a trump against 4♠ also. Moshe, East, figured that any minor suit tricks that the defense had coming were unlikely to disappear. But a heart trick might disappear if declarer had strong clubs.

So hoping to catch West with the ♡J, he shifted to the ♡10 at Trick 2. Dummy's ♡Q won, but when declarer drew the last trump and started clubs from the bottom, West won the second club and returned the ♡J to beat the contract.

DEAL 144. CREATING AN ENTRY FOR PARTNER

```
                        ♠ J 8
                        ♡ K Q 9 4
                        ◊ A Q J 10 8
                        ♣ 8 5
        ♠ K Q 10 7 5 3                      ♠ A
        ♡ 3                                 ♡ 7 6 2
        ◊ 5 2                               ◊ K 9 7 4
        ♣ 10 7 3 2                          ♣ K Q J 6 4
                        ♠ 9 6 4 2
                        ♡ A J 10 8 5
                        ◊ 6 3
                        ♣ A 9
```

After East opened 1♣ as dealer, South overcalled 1♡. North had no trouble bidding 4♡ over West's 2♠ (played as a weak jump response).

West led the ♠K. East overtook with the ♠A to shift to the ♣K, but South knew to duck. After winning the next club, South drew trump ending in hand and lost a diamond finesse. Now he was able to discard his three remaining spades on dummy's long diamonds. Making 4♡.

Might the defense have prevailed?

In the other room, West responded only 1♠, but the rest of the auction and the opening lead were the same.

Easter was approaching. East recalled the William Blake song, *The Lamb*, and thought, "May as well be hung for a sheep."

Accordingly, he shifted to the ♣6. South, Stella by Starlight, knew what was going on and deep-finessed the ♣9. But West won the ♣10 and continued spades. Down one.

Stella turned to East and muttered, "Lucky, lucky! I might have had the ten of clubs and made an overtrick."

"I'll worry about overtricks when I play matchpoints with my clients in the Big Room," he answered.

Printed in the United States
by Baker & Taylor Publisher Services